Decision Making
IN COMMUNITIES

Why groups of smart people
sometimes make bad decisions

By Jasmine Martirossian
Debra H. Lewin, Editor

Community Associations Press
Alexandria, VA

ISBN: 0-944715-62-1

Library of Congress Cataloging-in-Publication Data

Martirossian, Jasmine, 1968-
   Decision making in communities : why groups of smart people sometimes make bad
   decisions / by Jasmine Martirossian.
      p. cm.
   Includes bibliographical references.
   ISBN 0-944715-62-1 (alk. paper)
      1. Group decision making. I. Title.

   HM746 .M37 2001
   302.3--dc21

                                                            2001047097

Community Associations Press
A Division of Community Associations Institute
225 Reinekers Lane, Suite 300
Alexandria, VA 22314

Acknowledgments

I would very much like to thank the following individuals who gave their time and energies to review this book at different stages of its development.

Lief Carter, PhD
Boulder, CO

Marvin J. Nodiff, Esq.
St. Louis, MO

W. Stephen Castle, CMCA, AMS, PCAM
Plymouth Meeting, PA

Patricia Popovich
Alexandria, VA

Ellen Hirsch de Haan, Esq.
St. Petersburg, FL

Becky Smith, PhD
Reston, VA

Sandra K. Denton, CMCA, PCAM
Sugar Land, TX

Carolyn Vandam
Boston, MA

Erin Fuller
Alexandria, VA

Patricia A. Wasson, PCAM
Celebration, FL

Stephen Harvill, PCAM
Dallas, TX

Dave Wolfenden
Scottsdale, AZ

Stanley T. Myles
Washington, D.C.

I would like to extend special thanks to the editor, Debra Lewin, for her invaluable expertise and insights. Working with Debra has been a true joy and has made the process of editing enjoyable.

When a journalist pointed to a canvas and asked Pablo Picasso how long it had taken him to paint it, Picasso answered along the lines of forty years, nine months, three weeks, two days, seven hours, twenty minutes and ten seconds. He was joking, of course. The wisdom in this is that whatever we do at present, whatever we accomplish, is usually the result of our cumulative past experiences and interactions with others, and not a single person can claim exclusive credit for their accomplishments.

Hence, I would also like to thank some of the members of my primary group (you have to read the book to know what I mean). From my grandparents, aunts and uncles, and parents I have received the gift of love. And, while it's hard to recognize everyone by name, I have to mention my mom, Aelita Dolukhanian, and thank her for her immense protective love and for teaching me to recognize excellence and aspire to it. I would like to honor the memory of Lendrush Khurshudian and to thank him for teaching me to spread my wings and know that the impossible can be made possible. I would like to thank Leili Bagratuni for teaching me tolerance, and kindness. I would like to express my immense gratitude to Leonard Buckle and Suzann Thomas-Buckle for being the guiding lights on my life's path, for their love and unwavering faith in me. And for that, with the intent of acknowledging their many silent contributions to humanity, I dedicate this book to them.

Contents

Preface

Although I'm a lecturer at Northeastern University in Boston, Massachusetts, I'm writing this book on group dynamics for Community Associations Press because community associations and the Community Associations Institute (CAI) have become a major part of my life in the last few years. I'm presently a Trustee on CAI's Board of Trustees and a Director on the Board of Directors of the Community Associations Institute's Research Foundation, and I'm a frequent contributor to *Common Ground* magazine.

My research focuses on community associations, and my doctoral dissertation is on community associations. For my research, I had the honor of being granted the 1998 Byron Hanke Fellowship by the CAI Research Foundation. I have been a presenter at numerous CAI conferences around the United States, and I've had the privilege to interview hundreds of individuals from around the country who are involved with community associations either as residents or as professionals. Often, I use community associations as examples during my lectures at Northeastern University.

It was all this work as well as feedback from many individuals that led me to believe that a book on group dynamics exposing the workings of a group setting would be necessary and useful to both practitioners of community associations and residents alike.

I should tell you, though, that I still remember a time when I was not professionally involved in community associations and was a mere unit owner in a condominium. Trust me, when selecting my property I was not the least bit concerned with group dynamics in the association. I knew that I wanted to live in the Back Bay neighborhood of Boston, and, so, having found the right property, I quickly made an offer to buy. Anyone familiar with the Back Bay knows that much of this section of Boston consists of row houses or former hotels that have been split up and converted into condominiums. However, when I was first making my decision to buy, it was the location that was on my mind, not the fact that I would be purchasing a unit that was part of a shared common property owned by the condominium association.

A day before the closing date I made an effort to read the master deed and the bylaws of my condominium association. (I have since learned that only about ten percent of community association buyers actually take the time to read these documents before purchasing.) In my case, the document exceeded 120 pages.[1] I found clauses that didn't seem too attractive, at least to me, since, in my opinion, they gave too much leverage to the board of trustees. But the die was cast, and I would dutifully show up at my attorney's office the next day to sign the papers granting me the rights to the property.

Then, having moved in, for a while I guess I fit the profile of the average condominium owner who writes monthly checks to the association, but otherwise stays completely uninvolved. And then in November of 1995, around midnight, I got a phone call from the association's management company warning me that plumbers would soon be in my unit investigating a leak between the two floors. My bathroom was dry; I could neither see nor hear a leak; I confidently waited for the plumbers to show up.

Ten minutes later, two burly men pushed their way into the bathroom and—fully ignoring me—started discussing how they would dismantle the sink and drill underneath it to reach the (yet unidentified) leak. First, I observed their actions in silent horror, disbelieving my ears. When I asked their intentions, I found out that they didn't intend to ask my permission to proceed, because my property was part of the condominium association. The argument was simple, there was a leak, it needed to be fixed immediately, and the trustees had given the plumbers permission to act as they deemed appropriate.

At this point, I protested vigorously, pointing out that if the ceiling of the apartment below had already fallen out, as they told me, they should try to identify the source of the leak through that opening, instead of destroying more property and incurring greater expenses in fixing it. They looked at me as though I was completely clueless, and threatened to bring in the trustees at that late hour. I challenged them to do so, and told them they could not dismantle the sink. After a brief screaming match they left.

It turned out they went into another unit on my floor with bathroom walls adjacent to mine and drilled through there. Notably, the owners of this unit were out of town. With all the drilling and hammering next door it was a restless night, during which the realization sank in that this was the reality of belonging to a condominium association.

The monthly meeting of the board of trustees was the next aspect of condominium living to catch my attention. Usually, two or three days before a meeting, notices would go up in the lobby and in the elevator announcing the date and time of the upcoming meeting. Every now and then, on my way in and out of the building, I would see this group of people gathered in the lobby discussing what seemed like very mundane matters. I noticed that no residents, except for the board members themselves, ever observed or participated in these meetings.

And then, as I was walking by a meeting one day, I heard an engineer say that a project would cost one million dollars to complete. I realized that I—and all the other owners—would soon have a huge assessment for a project I knew nothing about. The next morning I rushed to ask our well-informed superintendent what this one million dollar expenditure was about, and found out that the parapet wall of this old, historic building, designed in the Moorish revival style, had disintegrated and needed to be redone. That's when I decided I wanted to have a say in the decision-making process. It was time to get elected.

I phoned one of the trustees, and she soon met me for an interview. She said it was remarkable that I was interested in the business of running the association. At the next rather uneventful annual meeting (with seven attendees), I was elected a trustee. At the next monthly board meeting, the all-female, four-member board elected me as chair. (I should note that group dynamics were at work, but I didn't think of this situation in those terms at that time.) I'd learn later that this was a very handy solution for a board that was unofficially divided into two camps—I came with no prior baggage and I was conveniently neutral. And, thus, the saga of my involvement with condominium issues began.

Had it not been for Prof. Suzann Thomas-Buckle's insightful observation and suggestion, I never would have considered condominium or community associations as a topic for my dissertation. Why? I guess because I lived there, and it was a subject too close to home. As philosopher Albert Borgmann once said about Montana, where he lives, "Why did I not find Montana interesting? I guess because I live there, because I know it too well. I guess because I take it for granted. But that's where the most interesting clues to our life are—in what we take for granted."

By now you have a sense how common my initial involvement with community associations was. However, what's not at all common is the importance that groups play in running a community association and ensuring—or sometimes getting in the way of—building a harmonious community. And, while this book is intended specifically for community associations and the professionals who support them, everyone can benefit from a knowledge of group influences on our decision-making processes.

In this book I've drawn on socio-psychological research to help explain why smart people sometimes make really stupid decisions. Hard as it is to accept, we aren't always guided by our independent thinking. All of us are very susceptible to situational influences, and within groups, the effects of these influences are amplified. Understanding those influences and group dynamics will help us become more effective as members of groups; and, in the case of community associations, this will enable us to be better trustees or directors, and to better understand what's at play in our communities.

I've used many examples of bad decisions that were made by community associations or by the professionals serving them. This is not to imply that bad decisions are the norm in community associations. Indeed, that isn't the case. There are thousands of associations where people make good decisions, build solid communities, and live in harmony. My hope is that this book will enable other associations to enjoy the same harmony. Once we understand the power and influences of social forces and the interactions occurring in groups, all of us can become more effective members of those groups.

Jasmine Martirossian
Summer 2001

CHAPTER 1

What is a Group?

People are fundamentally social creatures. Most of our experiences are social and occur within social settings, especially in groups. One can hardly overestimate the importance of groups in our lives.

Our involvement in groups starts at a very young age. Mothers eagerly enroll their toddlers in play groups. Then we move on to groups in our kindergartens, schools, neighborhoods, workplaces, and professional associations. From a very young age we learn to identify ourselves as part of different groups, and often our role within a given group becomes very closely tied to our identity.

When it comes to how we perform within a group, not all of us fare equally well. Some of our friends, colleagues, and relatives inevitably assume positions of leadership within groups, while others always stay on the edge of the group. Some of the people we know seem to always sway the opinion of the group and get the results they want, while others never quite succeed.

Why do some people fare better in groups than others? Being a highly individualist society, we often believe that those who do very well in groups succeed because of their individual qualities of excellence. However, this places too much importance on the powers of a given individual, and doesn't consider the influences coming directly from the group itself. Unlikely as it may seem, a host of group dynamics takes place within a group setting independent of our own behavior and responses. In fact, those dynamics often predicate, dictate, and shape our behavior and responses. Some people have intuitive skills that help them see the social interactions in a group, but most others have to learn them. Fortunately, social psychologists have done a lot of research that shows what dynamics of social interaction are at play in group settings.

Everyone knows, and even most children will say, that a group is more than one person. But it isn't quite that simple, so sociologists have provided the following definitions: "A social group is two or more people who identify and interact with one another";[2] or "A social group consists of two or more people who regularly interact and feel some sense of solidarity or common identity."[3]

Joseph Luft weighs in on this issue by identifying four major characteristics necessary to make a group a group:

1. Some interaction must take place.
2. Some purpose or goal must be shared.
3. Some differentiation of behavior or function must begin to emerge.
4. There must be more worth or value in being within the group than in being outside of it.[4]

All of these definitions clearly indicate that for a group to be a group its members must share a sense of belonging, a set of common interests, and a sense of familiarity with one another.

Aggregates

Do 50,000 screaming fans in a stadium cheering a football game comprise a group? Not according to the definition above. In fact, they're called aggregates, "collections of people who are physically at the same place at the same time, but do not interact in any meaningful way."[5] Aggregates contain people from all walks of life. For instance, the fans in the stadium will include physicians, community association managers, technicians, carpenters, plumbers, police officers, professors, and students. Although they're all in the same ballpark, each has a different social position. Thus, aggregates share common space, but not social status.

Aggregates are not considered groups. Yet they can turn into a group if their attention is unexpectedly focused on something specific—like an emergency. The most commonly cited example of such a case depicts people riding in the same elevator cabin. Usually, most people in elevators try to avoid eye contact and gaze intently at changing floor numbers, which I think is done exactly to avoid eye contact with others. However, should the elevator get stuck between floors, they will start engaging in small talk. Depending on how long they're confined, they may share life stories and deep secrets before they're freed. Clearly, the emergency will have turned them into a group.

The same thing is true in community associations. Most people would like to be members of a community, but the reality is they live in the community as aggregates rather than as group members. They are simply sharing common space and paying their monthly fees to continue being in that space, just as football fans pay for tickets to be in the stadium. However, should a contentious issue arise affecting all or part of the community association, residents will quickly form groups.

Categories

Unlike aggregates—that share space, but not social status—*categories* of people share social status, but not space. For instance, students, homeowners, condominium dwellers, Beatles fans, physicians, professors, community association managers, Roman Catholics, people with green eyes, and insurance agents are all categories of people. Like aggregates, categories can turn into groups, especially if what they have in common is challenged or threatened.

Usually, categories will turn into groups by forming affiliations with organizations. For instance, physicians act as a group through the American Medical Association. Likewise, community association managers act as a group through their membership in the Community Associations Institute or through local managers' associations.

Often categories of people will mobilize their resources and turn into groups even in cases where their sense of belonging to a certain category was not the basis of their identity. Homeowners are a good example of this. Most people owning homes do not introduce themselves in public as homeowners (unless they're attending a CAI conference). However, if a law is passed affecting all condominium owners in a given state, for example, then it's likely condominium owners will form interest-based groups. Homeownership will then become an identity-defining category, something that will focus people's attention.

Community associations are interesting social organizations because residents are simultaneously categories, aggregates, and groups of people. These terms may sound too academic, and it may seem that they're of relevance only to sociologists. Nonetheless, we have certain expectations that go with these terms, even if we don't use them. For instance, a major community association marketing message is that owners will be provided with care-free living—someone else will take care of the lawn, maintain the septic system, and clean the common areas. This sets people up to behave like aggregates, just like the people who buy tickets to attend a football game, and not like group members living in a tightly knit community. In contrast, co-housing properties, from the very beginning, place great emphasis on individual participation and contribution to the well-being and vitality of their community—thus setting up residents to behave like group members.

Primary and Secondary Groups

Groups may provide greater levels of intimacy and more intense interaction than aggregates or categories of people, but groups are not all equal nor do they have the same intra-group dynamics. In fact, they come in many shapes and forms and have many different characteristics. For example, one distinction is that groups can be either *primary* or *secondary*.

Charles Horton Cooley defined this distinction as early as 1909. He wrote, "By primary groups I mean those characterized by intimate face-to-face association and cooperation. They are primary in several senses, but chiefly in that they are fundamental in forming the social nature and ideals of the individual. The result of intimate association, psychologically, is a certain fusion of individualities in a common whole, so that one's very self, for many purposes at least, is the common life and purpose of the group. Perhaps the

The Co-housing Community

Co-housing emphasizes the social aspects of belonging to a community. It uses consensus as a tool for decision making, very rarely resorting to voting. In contrast to traditional forms of common interest communities that, unless they're very small, govern by representation, in co-housing everyone is a member of the governing board regardless of the size of the association.

According to The Co-housing Network, the official organization of co-housing associations in the United States, "Co-housing is the name of a type of collaborative housing that attempts to overcome the alienation of modern subdivisions in which no one knows their neighbors, and there is no sense of community."

Most co-housing projects are developed from scratch, while some are retrofitted. In the latter case houses are gradually bought in an existing neighborhood and converted to fit the needs of co-housers. N Street Co-housing in Davis, California, is a classic example of retrofitting.

Even though there's no standard cookie-cutter format for co-housing projects, most of them share a number of characteristics. Between 20 and 30 single-family homes are clustered around a courtyard, or these homes may be located on a pedestrian street leading to the common facilities. Architecture plays a pivotal role in cementing the sense of community among co-housers. For instance, parking facilities often are peripherally located to foster interaction between the residents as they make their daily trek from the parking lot to their homes.

High-rise co-housing projects already exist in Sweden, where the government had built an excessive number of high-rise buildings in the '60s and '70s, while Denmark has a number of co-housing developments with only 8 or 10 units.

In co-housing, the common facilities often include a common dining room and a kitchen for the preparation of common meals, as well as children's play areas, woodworking shops and the like. Members of the community expect to share many items such as lawn mowers, tools, and toys.

simplest way of describing this wholeness is by saying it is a 'we'; it involves the sort of sympathy and mutual identification for which 'we' is the natural expression. One lives in the feeling of the whole and finds the chief aims of his will in that feeling."[6] The level of closeness described by Cooley is experienced in cases where people associate with one another closely, intimately, and frequently.

Primary Groups

The family is the most profound example of a primary group. They're comfortable enough with one another to share confidences and secrets, and they're usually very loyal to the other members of the group. In essence, "primary groups are an end in themselves, not a means to an end."[7]

Primary groups don't always strive towards harmony. Just the opposite may, in fact, be true. They may engage in intense competition and passionate disagreements. However, what sets primary groups apart is that "these passions are socialized by sympathy, and come, or tend to come, under the discipline of a common spirit."[8] This common spirit allows primary groups to successfully weather their disputes and disagreements.

Secondary Groups

If primary groups are characterized by their focus on intimacy, trust, and emotional involvement, secondary groups are characterized by their focus on a common goal. Secondary groups are, in many ways, the opposite of primary groups. "The secondary group is a large and impersonal social group whose members pursue a specific goal or activity. . . . Secondary relationships involve weak emotional ties and little personal knowledge of one another."[9] Throughout our lives we go in and out of many secondary groups. For instance, most classrooms, workplaces, parent-teacher associations, homeowners associations, and church and synagogue congregations are forms of secondary groups.

Over time, certain parts of secondary groups can turn into primary groups. Let's say a few employees in a large corporation are assigned to be members of a team. Their intense work experience may create life-long bonds. Years later when they are all employed elsewhere, they still meet regularly and sometimes vacation together—their secondary group has clearly become a primary group. In general, secondary groups are not an end in themselves, rather they are a means to an end.

In-Groups and Out-Groups

Remember high school with its factions, including the popular people, the nerds, the jocks, and the freaks? The terminology may have been different in your high school, but the factions were there regardless. High school factions epitomize in-groups and out-groups. "An *in-group* is a social group commanding a member's esteem and loyalty. An *out-group*, by contrast, is a social group toward which one feels competition or opposition. In-groups and out-groups are based on the idea that 'we' have valued traits that 'they' lack."[10]

Community conflicts can create marginalized and rather well-defined in-groups and out-groups. In one community factions emerged because some residents were feeding stray cats and others objected. Some communities even end up giving these groups unofficial names—often pejorative—just like in high school. The cat lovers began referring to those who objected to feeding strays as The Anti-Cats. This is deplorable and only aggravates the conflict,

The Way We Weren't

Is your community association a primary group? Is it a place where people associate with one another closely, intimately, and frequently? Is it disciplined by a common spirit that allows it to weather disagreements? No? Why not? Everyone agrees that neighborhoods *used to be* primary groups and that the sense of community was strong.

Consider this quote: "In our own life the intimacy of the neighborhood has been broken up by the growth of an intricate mesh of wider contacts which leaves us strangers to people who live in the same house. And even in the country the same principle is at work, though less obviously, diminishing our economic and spiritual community with our neighbors."[11]

Did these words come from a modern-day newspaper lamenting our loss of neighborliness and community? No, they were written in 1909—a time that, according to present popular beliefs, had a much stronger sense of neighborliness and community.

So how can we explain the discrepancy?

Each generation bemoans the loss of community and neighborliness as it grows older, because, over time, nostalgic images replace what we actually experienced. For example, "When schoolchildren return from vacation and are asked to list the good things and the bad things about their summer, their lists tend to be equally long. Over the year, however, if the exercise is repeated, the good list grows longer and the bad shorter until by the end of the year the children are describing not actual vacations but idealized images of Vacation."[12] This is often exactly the way we remember communities. This tends to set the bar too high for judging communities' standards and performance, which may lead to discounting many positive accomplishments that do exist in modern-day communities.

but in-groups and out-groups will probably always exist wherever you have a lot of people.

Many people find psychic satisfaction in belonging to an in-group; in fact, for many, an in-group can serve as a primary group. For these people finding and belonging to an in-group can be a lifelong quest. People tend to believe the qualities at which they excel are better and more desirable than qualities they don't possess, and they're attracted to others with the same qualities and especially values.

Hence, it isn't difficult to understand why a community can become easily divided into in-groups and out-groups if a major conflict erupts. A successful community might attempt to define the entire community as an in-group. However, if the community is an in-group, who and where is the out-group?

Community Associations as Reference Groups

In a community association, the governing documents explicitly define the reference group by mandating colors of paint and window treatments, limiting the number of pets, specifying where children may play, and so on. Many a court case has revolved around residents and owners who have rebelled against these restrictions and refused to abide by them. However, restrictive as this may sound, community associations as defined reference groups are very attractive to Americans because they offer the rare qualities of certainty and predictability in an age of rapid and incessant change.

One problem that occurs in community associations is that a group of people, usually the elected leaders, reifies the governing documents or the Covenants, Conditions and Restrictions (CC&Rs). Reification means treating an immaterial object or idea as if it had concrete or material existence. In such a case, rules and regulations become untouchable, sovereign members of the community. People forget that they make the rules and that they can change them if the standards and interests of this reference group shift.

This issue brings many gated communities and even co-housing developments under criticism regarding their real or perceived separation from the rest of the community or society.

Take any community conflict and it might be easy to see how people's loyalties often accompanied by their actions fall along the conflict's fault lines separating the in-groups and out-groups.

And while in-groups and out-groups are not likely to wither away any time soon, it is helpful to have an awareness of them.

Reference Groups

Reference groups serve as benchmarks for us to assess our own performance or behavior. They serve "two closely related but distinct functions: a *normative* function of providing guidance concerning how to act, and a *comparative* function whereby we assess ourselves in relation to others. When these functions are provided by a single person, we call that individual a *role model.*"[13]

Whether we realize it or not, we constantly compare ourselves to reference groups and we follow unwritten social rules as a result. For example, when a family that has never lived in the suburbs buys a suburban home, one thing they're likely to do is mow the lawn—even if they've never had a lawn and personally prefer the look of wilderness. Why? Because their neighbors—the reference group—have manicured lawns, and they have provided guidance on how to act. So, when our family mows the lawn they're demonstrating the "normal" behavior of the reference group.

Reference groups also serve a comparative function—that is, they give us something to compare ourselves to. In the case of our suburban family, the comparative function will kick in if they decide to have the best lawn in the neighborhood and make great effort to create it. The phenomenon known as Keeping Up With the Joneses is an example of the comparative function of reference groups carried to extremes.

We can be either within our reference group, as is the case with members in a community association or residents in a neighborhood, or we can be outside the reference group, as is the case with boys emulating their favorite athletes. Either way, reference groups play an important social function: they provide a sense of comfort because they set guidelines of how to act and behave, thus stimulating social change by inspiring people to greater heights and achievements.

CHAPTER 2

What is Group Dynamics?

G roups are "fluid"—they're constantly changing and transforming themselves. Realizing this can help many people cope with the changes that occur in groups. Unfortunately, some individuals may get used to and internalize the specific way a group functions, and then once changes occur, these people have difficulties in the new group. A good example of this is when a community association's board acquires a few new members following the annual election. Let's say, if they had seven members, and three of them are new, the three new individuals may dramatically alter the dynamics of group interaction on the board. If the four incumbents do not deal well with this process of transition, much turmoil may occur. One thing to keep in mind about any group is that it is "a living system, self-regulating through shared perception and interaction, sensing, and feedback, and through interchange with its environment."[14] All of these aspects that contribute to changes in a group are controlled by group dynamics.

"Group dynamics" is a catchy term, but what does it actually mean? The word dynamics "implies forces that are complex and interdependent in a common field or setting."[15] As for group dynamics, it is a "field of inquiry dedicated to advancing knowledge about the nature of groups, the laws of their development, and their interrelations with individuals, other groups, and larger institutions."[16] Researchers have studied many aspects of group dynamics, and the most important ones seem to be size, composition, leadership, conformity within the group, and decision making.

Group Size

Does group size matter? Yes! How many times have you commented on the size of a group you were part of? Sometimes you may have sighed and said that too many cooks spoil the broth, thinking that the group was too big. Other times you may have felt constrained by how small a group was.

Pay attention to how people behave at a party when the first few people have just arrived. John Macionis observes that "until about six people enter the room, everyone generally shares a single conversation. But as more people arrive, the group soon divides into two or more clusters. Size plays a crucial role in how group members interact."[17]

Dyads

The smallest group consists of two people and is called a dyad, which means "pair" in Greek.[18] Married couples, lovers, and best friends are good examples of dyads. Because we tend to experience some of our most intense and intimate relationships as dyads, dyads are very desirable. Indeed, most people spend much of their lives seeking the perfect dyadic relationship.

People in dyadic relationships often engage in heroic acts for the sake of each other, and much of the world's literature either sings praises to or laments the trials and tribulations of a dyadic relationship; "Romeo and Juliet," for example, does both.

On the other hand, dyadic relationships with a strong sense of parity and equality can be plagued with indecision and caught in a state of paralysis because each member can veto the decisions or block the moves of the other. This happens in the rare situations when a condominium association consists of only two units. If the two neighbors get along and like each other, peace will prevail. However, there is also room for misery and litigation if one of the members turns down the other neighbor's proposals.

Dyadic relationships can provide a safe haven, but they can also allow people to behave deplorably, making the relationship vulnerable, volatile, and unreliable. People will abuse their partners psychologically, physically, and mentally, they will abandon them at critical times, and sometimes will make no effort to save a relationship. In the United States one of every two first marriages ends in divorce. In short, dyads are the best of relationships and the worst of relationships.

Triads

A triad, a group of three people, moves away from the immediate and intense intimacy of a dyad. However, it compensates with greater stability. In family settings, first children can be stabilizers. A triad is more stable than a dyad because one member can act as a mediator if relations between the other two become strained.[19] But triads are not always nice or harmonious. Sometimes two members of the triad may form a strong alliance and leave the third feeling like a sleeve for a vest.

As group size grows, intimacy decreases and stability increases. Diminished intimacy creates a need for more formalized relations within the group. "People address larger groups rather than talking to them conversationally."[20] This is representative of the changing dynamics within the group.

More than Two or Three

As groups grow the number of relationships within them increases geometrically. If, in a dyad, there are two participants and one relationship and, in a triad, there are three participants and three relationships, one would think that with four participants there would be four relationships. However, there are actually six relationships in a group of four people.

This increase in the number of relationships has an astonishing effect as groups get larger. For instance, in a group with five people there are ten relationships, while in a group of seven people there are 21 relationships. Therefore, groups that are too large and have a multitude of relationships may ultimately become unwieldy and break down into factions.

Group size and communication within the group have an inverse relationship—the larger the group becomes, the less communication occurs within the group. "A smaller percentage of individuals contribute to group discussions. This is apparently due both to the members' heightened fear of participation, and to the simple fact that there is less time for individuals to express themselves in large gatherings."[21]

Multiplying Relationships

As groups grow, the number of relationships within them increases geometrically.

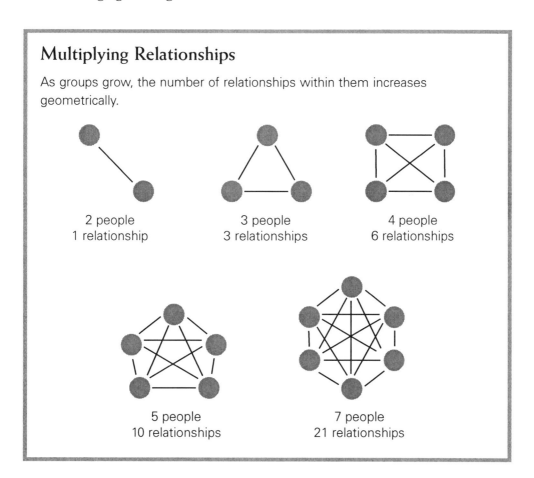

2 people
1 relationship

3 people
3 relationships

4 people
6 relationships

5 people
10 relationships

7 people
21 relationships

Group Composition

The composition of a group—that is, the nature and background of its members—can affect the dynamics within the group. One aspect of group composition is that they are either heterogeneous or homogeneous.

Heterogeneous groups are made up of people with disparate and dissimilar backgrounds. Homogeneous groups comprise people with very similar backgrounds. What's similar about group members' backgrounds can cut across a variety of social issues. For instance, community association managers and recovering alcoholics would each be considered homogeneous groups.

Samuel T. Gladding believes that "heterogeneous groups can broaden members' horizons and enliven interpersonal interactions. Such groups may be helpful in problem solving . . . homogeneous groups are extremely beneficial in working through specific issues. Task/work groups are often homogeneous for this reason. The nature and purpose of the group usually determines what its member composition will be."[22]

Thus, for the sake of a well-governed and well-managed community association, perhaps boards should be heterogeneous groups and committees should be homogeneous groups. A heterogeneous board will be more successful in evaluating a variety of options and considering a panoply of choices, while a homogeneous committee will be more adept at dealing with their specific task. An ideal board would reflect the community's diversity, and it would draw on people of different ages and with different professional affiliations. On the other hand, the ideal committee, say, a decorating committee, would draw on people who have related expertise.

"Heterogeneous groups turn outward. The more internally diverse a group is, the more likely its members are to interact with outsiders."[23] Thus, a heterogeneous board is more likely to succeed at reaching out to association members, strengthening a sense of community, and increasing levels of community participation.

Group Leadership

"Leadership is the process by which certain individuals mobilize and guide groups."[24] It is not only one of the most complex and desirable roles in society, leadership is also one of the most important elements influencing group dynamics.

Leadership isn't a one-size-fits-all quality; for example, it can be situational. Some people are successful leaders in one setting and fail totally in another. For instance, a person who runs a major manufacturing plant may not necessarily be a good community leader, and vice versa.

Although leadership is an important factor for achieving harmony in a community, few people think about the group dynamics on the association's board or the associated leadership issues when buying into a community association, especially if they're first-time buyers. However, it's conceivable that someone moving from a dysfunctional association might have such questions on their minds.

Types of Leaders in Small Groups

Two distinct leadership types are associated with small groups—task (or instrumental) leadership and social (or expressive) leadership, which is also known as group-maintenance leadership. As the name suggests, task leaders focus on completing specific goals, while social leaders inspire and motivate the group in general.

Task or instrumental leaders' functions include:[25]

- helping set and clarify goals
- focusing on information needed
- drawing on available group resources
- stimulating research
- maintaining orderly operating procedures
- introducing suggestions when they are needed
- establishing an atmosphere that permits testing
- rigorously evaluating ideas
- devoting oneself to the task
- attending to the clock and the schedule
- pulling the group together for consensus or patterns of action
- enabling the group to determine and evaluate its progress

Social or expressive leaders' functions include:[26]

- encouraging participation by everyone in the group
- keeping everyone in a friendly mood
- responding to the emotional concerns of group members when that is appropriate
- promoting open communication
- listening attentively to all contributions
- encouraging with positive feedback
- showing enthusiasm and good humor
- promoting pride in the group
- judging accurately the changing moods of the group
- providing productive outlets for tensions

Leadership Styles

There are three major leadership styles—authoritarian, democratic, and laissez-faire (from the French phrase "allow [them] to do," implying noninterference in the affairs of others).

Authoritarian leaders usually take charge and personally control situations; they are very directive and insist on strict accountability from the group mem-

---

An Autocrat in Democratic Clothing

As part of my research, I have been observing many condominium boards for a number of years, and on one board a young man became chair who clearly fit the description of an authoritarian leader—he didn't seek others' input, he shot down others' ideas, gave assignments to everybody and demanded strict accountability. Above all, things would only get done the way he wanted them to be done. Private comments soon began to circulate about his leadership style, and he became aware that people were displeased that he didn't allow them to participate or provide input. He decided to change.

This young man now solicited input from every member of this seven-person board. However, he was still determined to have things done his way, so he would spend hours manipulating the situation so that his viewpoint would prevail. As a result, this board went from meeting once a month for two-to-three hours to meeting biweekly for four hours.

It was obvious the president was going through the motions of a democratic process that merely masked his autocratic leadership style. —jm

---

bers. In general, decisions are reached quickly without much input from the group. Although these attributes don't necessarily make authoritarian leaders very popular with the group, the groups are usually productive and do well in a crisis. Authoritarian leaders tend to be more task-oriented than expressive leaders. Authoritarian leaders in community associations are the board presidents who dominate the group unconditionally, insist on doing things their way, and shoot down without a second thought other members' ideas they don't like.

Democratic leaders, unlike authoritarian leaders, rely more on group participation and input. They draw heavily on the ideas of the members of the group, and spend a lot of time in group discussion. This style of leadership is less effective in a crisis, yet democratic leaders win far more affection from their group members. Community association boards that have a democratic leader tend to be very happy with their working relationship on the board, and tend to feel listened to and appreciated. Still, having a democratic leader doesn't guarantee a successful outcome for the board. Sometimes too much emphasis on group process may come at the expense of reaching productive outcomes. In essence, the process inadvertently becomes the goal and product of the group.

Laissez-faire leaders are very hands-off and, in general, fail to provide any clear sense of direction to the group members. Their approach allows matters to take their natural course, and this may not necessarily have an advantageous outcome. Laissez-faire leaders neither discourage nor encourage group participation, nor do they make any effort to motivate the group. Sometimes in this process another group leader may emerge. Laissez-faire leadership is not conducive to group productivity, and is perhaps the least desirable style of leadership. Unfortunately, many community association boards function in this way.

Despite these categorizations, most of the time there are few clear and distinct leadership types functioning. Most groups will go through periods of leadership that might fit any of the three leadership styles.

The difference in the results that autocratic and democratic leaders get isn't very clear. In fact, a recent study concluded that neither is more productive than the other, but that democratic leaders have more satisfied groups.[27]

Many studies on leadership have compared "permissive, follower-oriented, participative, and considerate leadership styles with restrictive, task-oriented, directive, socially distant, and structured leadership styles."[28] A review of these studies showed that "Person-oriented styles of leadership are not consistently related to productivity. Among the work-oriented leadership styles, socially distant, directive, and structured leader behaviors that tend to maintain role differentiation and let members know what to expect are consistently related to group productivity. Among the person-oriented leadership styles, only those providing for member participation in decision making and showing concern for members' welfare and comfort are consistently related to group cohesiveness. Among the work-oriented leadership styles, only the structuring of member expectations is uniformly related to group cohesiveness. All of the person-oriented leadership styles tend to be related to member satisfaction. Only the structuring of member expectations is related positively to member satisfaction among the work-oriented leadership styles."[29]

Get the Job Done or Keep the Group Happy?

People-Oriented Leaders

Characteristics:	*Accomplishments:*
■ Permissive	■ Group is not always productive
■ Follower-oriented	■ Group is cohesive
■ Participative	■ Group is satisfied
■ Considerate	

Task-Oriented Leaders

Characteristic:	*Accomplishments*
■ Restrictive	■ Group is productive
■ Task-oriented	■ Group is cohesive only when members know exactly what to expect
■ Directive	
■ Socially distant	■ Group is satisfied only when members know exactly what to expect
■ Structured	

Leaders who clearly define their roles and what they expect from the members of the group and who are concerned for the well being and contributions of the group may be the most effective.

Thus, a democratic leadership style is highly desirable for community associations since it yields high member satisfaction—a major factor in community harmony. It's also an important consideration when working with volunteer boards. And yet, the work-oriented aspects of the autocratic leadership style are essential if projects are to be completed in the association. After all, it's more likely that residents will complain about an unfinished paint job than about the lack of community harmony.

Hence, successful leaders of community associations will merge the democratic and autocratic leadership styles. They will solicit everyone's input, but also clearly assign roles and responsibilities for board and committee members. They will clearly define what they expect and hold board members accountable.

Group Conformity

Few Americans see themselves as conformists. Rather, they think of themselves as independent individuals who wouldn't be swayed by group pressures. This image is the logical result of an American culture that values individualism as an absolute virtue. Individualism is instilled by parents and reinforced by an educational system that encourages children to think independently and be aware of their individuality.

However, despite a strong sense of individuality, we cave in to group pressures every day. For example, imagine you have just watched a new movie with a group of friends. They all loved it, but you didn't. Isn't it likely that you may end up claiming that you liked the movie? At this point, you're protesting that you wouldn't cave in, you'd voice your opinions regardless of what the group said. And in many cases it may be so. However, we shouldn't discount the extent to which groups breed conformity.

Solomon Asch devised a simple, but groundbreaking, experiment that demonstrated the power of group conformity.[30] He set up a simple room containing little more than a long table and two charts. The first chart depicted a single line. The second chart had three lines marked A, B, and C. One of the three lines on the second chart was obviously the same length as the single line on the first chart. He seated a group of six to eight strangers at the table facing the charts and asked them to state which line on the second chart matched the single line on the first chart. With group after group, the participants' responses were 100 percent correct.

Then Asch changed a small element in his experiment. He seated a group of strangers around the table and asked all but one person to identify the wrong line. That one person was seated next to last at the table and was the one actually being tested. With group after group, an amazing thing started to happen, one-third of the test subjects went along with the group and named the wrong line as the matching one.

One in every three individuals caved in to group pressure simply to avoid deviating from what seemed to be group consensus! In interviews after the experiment Asch found that "almost all the conformers knew they were answering incorrectly but were not willing to openly defy the expressed opinion of the rest of the group."[31] If people conform so easily to a group of strangers, how much more easily will they conform to familiar groups such as friends, family, neighbors, and, of course, community association boards?

Compared to the simple elegance of Asch's experiment, Stanley Milgram's experiments on authority are far more complex, but they demonstrate the same principles of group conformity.

Milgram recruited people to participate in a study on memory and learning. Ostensibly, this process was to measure the effects of punishment on learning. Recruits might play the role of teacher or learner, and a drawing was used to decide who was which. However, it was rigged so that the recruit was always the "teacher." The learner was always a 47-year-old Irish-American accountant whom most people found likable. After the drawing people were taken "to an adjacent room and the learner was strapped into an 'electric chair'. . . ."[32]

The role of the experimenter was played by a 31-year-old high school biology teacher—deliberately dressed in a lab coat to make him look official—who told the "teacher" that the "learner" was strapped into the "electric chair" so that he couldn't move much when he received the electric shocks. The teacher was told to administer the electricity if the learner made any mistakes during the lesson.

The teacher was told to read several pairs of words to the student, then repeat the first word in a pair expecting the student to correctly identify the second word in the pair. If the learner made mistakes about the second word—and he was told to deliberately make them—the teacher was to administer increasing levels of electric shock to the learner. The recruits were told by the white-coated experimenter to begin at 15 volts and increase incrementally to 450 volts.

The "shock generator" was labeled "Shock Generator, Type ZLB, Dyson Instrument Company, Waltham, Mass. Output 15 Volts–450 Volts";[33] but, in reality, the learner never received any shocks, even though he would playact pain and beg for mercy as increasing levels of shock were administered. Despite his moans, screams, and pounding, "none of the forty [teachers] during the initial research even questioned the procedure before reaching 300 volts, and twenty-six of [the teachers]—almost two-thirds—went all the way to 450 volts. The startling results show just how readily ordinary people obey authority figures."[34]

What does obedience to authority figures have to do with group conformity? Stanley Milgram asked the same question. Would the "teacher's" behavior change if he were acting as part of a group? To find out, he formed a group of three "teachers"—two were collaborating with him and following his instructions, while only one was actually being tested. This time the teachers were each told to suggest an appropriate shock level when the learner made a mistake, and "the group would then administer the lowest of the three suggestions. This arrangement gave the naïve subject the power to deliver a lesser shock regardless of what the others proposed. . . . The result was that the subjects applied voltage three to four times higher than other subjects did when acting alone in control conditions."[35] The test subject's unwillingness to be outdone by others in the group drove him to extremes. This illustrates how groups can actually affect our individual behaviors, sometimes making us do things that we wouldn't ordinarily do with as much zeal.

CHAPTER 3

Decision Making in Groups

Popular wisdom and an old cliché tell us that two heads are better than one, and lead us to think that when more than one person contributes to the process, together they make a better decision. Does that imply that the greater the number of people involved, the better the decision? That seems to be the popular perception. Consider, for instance, the mutual fund companies that emphasize in their marketing literature and public relations campaigns that teams of experts—not individual experts—manage their mutual funds. They are capitalizing on the strength of this perception.

People in some community associations also share the perception that group decision making is superior. For instance, one condominium association board was determined that all decisions, even those regarding the most minor issues, be ratified by the entire seven-person board. They refused to call the board president a president, or even a chair, adamantly insisting on "point-person," as the acceptable term. They specified that this person would be a mere conduit for communicating with the management company and would have absolutely no leeway for individual decision making—even in the most trivial matters.

But if groups make better decisions than individuals, why is individual decision making a highly valued social function? For instance, why is it that the more decision-making power that's associated with a given job, the better the compensation?

How Do Groups Influence Decision Making?

Let's just assume for now that groups do make better decisions. What is "better"? To answer that, let's also assume that "better decisions" are those limiting risk and increasing caution.

To find out if groups actually make decisions that are cautious and relatively risk free, social psychologists have conducted experiments and found that—interestingly—groups make decisions that both limit risk and increase risk, and that both effects are valid and are to be expected as outcomes of group decisions.

Group Decisions Increase Risk

James Stoner wrote up a number of real-life scenarios that called for making drastic decisions and taking risks. In his experiments, he asked *individual* test subjects to read these scenarios and assess the risk that should be taken on a scale of 1 to 10. Then he presented the same scenarios to *groups* of test subjects, once again asking them to make a decision and rate the level of risk that should be taken.

Stoner's experiments turned popular belief on its head. In his experiments, people actually increased their level of risk when they were making a decision as members of a group, and they were less willing to take risk when making a decision on their own. His experiments found that "group decisions [are] significantly more risky than the mean of the individual group members' prior decisions."[36] This phenomenon came to be known as the "risky shift."

Group Decisions Limit Risk

Shortly after Stoner's experiments, researchers Marquis and Nordhoy conducted a series of similar experiments that produced the opposite result. They found "evidence [supporting the idea] that group discussion might also lead to more cautious decisions."[37] This means that people in groups also make decisions that are more cautious than decisions they would make on their own.

In light of these findings, what should a community association manager or board member do when working with groups? The logical answer is: gauge the possible outcome based on group discussion and decide which direction the decision will swing—in the direction of increased or decreased risk? In order to do this, you need to understand group polarization.

Group Polarization

The puzzle of these opposite outcomes was solved with the discovery of a phenomenon called "group polarization," which reflects "a tendency for group discussion to *enhance* the individuals' initial leanings."[38] This means that if a person goes into a group discussion with a specific opinion on an issue, that individual's position will be enhanced by the time the group meeting is over. James Stoner summarizes his research in the following way, "For items on which the widely held values favored the risky alternative and on which the subjects considered themselves relatively risky, unanimous group decisions were more risky than the average of the initial individual decisions. The group decisions tended to be more cautious on items for which widely held values favored the cautious alternative and on which subjects consider themselves relatively cautious."[39]

For example, in a condominium association where lighting was insufficient, the board had to decide whether to replace the exterior lights at association expense with modern fixtures—which they would also have to main-tain—or at county expense with standard fixtures supplied and maintained by the local utility company. The association had budgeted for the modern fix-tures, and the residents wanted them because they were more attractive and provided more light. However, the board suspected that future maintenance costs might burden the association's resources or require a dues increase. During the discussion, individual board members said, "If it were just me, I'd get the attractive fixtures, and figure out later how to pay for the upkeep." But in the end, they voted for the county owned and maintained "institutional style" lights—a position favored strongly by one member who represented the community's fiscal conservatism.

Too Much Invested To Quit

Along with group polarization, groups also experience the "too much invested to quit" phenomenon that has cost many businesses huge sums of money.[40]

For instance, in one experiment Canadian business students were asked to make a decision on investing in a business that had a track record of failures: "72 percent [of students who] reinvested said they would seldom have invested if they were considering it as a new investment on its own merits; when mak-ing the same decision in groups, 94 percent opted for reinvestment."[41] Once again, decision making within the group setting had risk-taking outcomes.

Most of us are familiar with this phenomenon—indeed we talk about it everyday. We say we're "throwing good money after bad," when we have too much invested to quit—or we "get out while the getting's good." And, if the getting out isn't good, we "cut our losses." It's likely we've all experienced it at one time or another as private citizens, professionals, or members of a commu-nity association board.

For instance, a condominium association board had hired a superintendent who, after his first three months of stellar performance, totally slacked off. Yet for the next two years, although the board constantly debated what to do with him, they gave him three pay raises, two extra weeks of vacation, a better health insurance policy, and finally determined that this superintendent was not the right fit for the association. They had become the victims of the "too-much-invested-to-quit" phenomenon because they felt that they had already spent considerable amounts of time searching to fill this job, and did not want to feel as if they had wasted resources.

In another example, the president of a community association management company had a client association that, in the past seven years, had contracted with three management companies that collectively provided eight community association managers. Obviously, the association management company that could satisfy this association hasn't been created yet, and the association manag-er that could make this board happy hasn't been born. Nevertheless, this association management company president made an obvious effort to honor his professional commitment, and he tried to please this association at all costs.

However, the group polarization phenomenon and the too-much-invested-to-quit phenomenon were very much at work. As the real or perceived disputes deepened, each side became more entrenched in their original position, yet neither side was willing to end the relationship because each was too invested in the situation to quit. Generally, it's a good idea to cut your losses in situations like this at the time when you feel that, had you known then what you know now, you wouldn't have invested in it in the first place.

Group Polarization in Communities

The effects of group polarization are all around us, in varied social situations, and can often be observed in communities. "During community conflicts, like-minded people increasingly associate with one another. This amplifies their shared tendencies."[42]

Elvira Jackson, and her neighbors, tell a story of "a long, convoluted conflict that seems to never end"[43] that illustrates community polarization perfectly. Elvira lives in a community association in Mt. Imaginario, California, where she introduced me to several of her neighbors, two former community association board presidents, and one of the original combatants.

The conflict started about seven years ago between two couples: Ed and Melanie, and Gilda and her husband. Ed and Melanie, presently retired engineers, were members of the association's seven-member board. Depending on who's telling the story, they supposedly either left a ditch open or didn't light it sufficiently one Halloween weekend. No injuries resulted, but Gilda and her husband saw this as an opportunity to oust Ed and Melanie from the board. They accused them of gross negligence and the power struggle began.

Although Gilda's husband became president of the board, many residents agree that Gilda was actually running the show. I think this is probably true because I was struck in my conversations with the residents by the fact that no one used this man's proper name, everybody referred to him simply as "Gilda's husband," and some even had a hard time recalling his name. I later found out that his name was Greg.

This association is located in the heart of Silicon Valley, and it has seen a tremendous upsurge in property values in recent years. Long-time residents have seen prices skyrocket, but not necessarily their incomes. People who paid about $200,000 for a house in 1995 could sell it in 2001 for $700,000. On the other hand, half of the properties in this association have changed hands many times and brought in new owners with higher incomes—which may have contributed to a sense of division in the community. Additionally, the side that newcomers take in The Conflict has become a way to build identity in this community association.

Today Gilda and her husband are gone; they sold their unit and moved away a year ago, but the community is still divided on everything, no matter how trivial. Amazingly, the original issue is a distant memory.

While the scope of this book does not allow me to provide a detailed analysis of the evolution of this conflict, it's clearly a good example of the effect of group polarization run amok within a community association.

Discussion is a key element in the process of group polarization. Indeed, the importance of group discussions and the effect of polarization during community conflicts were confirmed by Coleman's field research on intergroup polarization during community conflicts: "Group discussion . . . is such an important phenomenon in community controversies that in the case of studies examined most descriptions of behavior during the intense part of the controversy were descriptions of discussion and of attempts to persuade or reinforce opinion."[44] Basically, the gist of this conclusion is that discussion does matter, and it can make or break the sense of harmony within a community.

As polarization increases in a community, so does "homogeneous grouping." This means that like-minded people come closer together strengthening their sense of being the in-group, clearly distinct from the other side—the outgroup. Research on community conflict has shown that "homogeneous grouping was a source of community polarization and the occurrence of social conflict further heightened."[45]

What Causes Group Polarization?

We have established that group polarization is a real phenomenon and part of life in a community, but what makes group polarization a reality? Simply stated: two things—information and a desire to be accepted. Social psychologists refer to these two influences as informational and normative. Informational influence "results from accepting evidence about reality," while normative influence is "based on a person's desire to be accepted or admired by others."[46]

Martin F. Kaplan argues that "informational influence implies that judgments, whether before or after discussion, are based on information about the issue. If judgments shift, it is because one has incorporated new information that was provided during discussion. This information can be provided forcefully, through persuasive arguments, or passively, via information sharing."[47] It follows that processing information is a very relevant part of group decision-making processes. However, groups may not process all information equally.

First, as group discussion ensues, it "elicits a pooling of ideas, most of which favor the dominant viewpoint. Ideas that were common knowledge to group members will often be brought up in discussion or, even if unmentioned, will jointly influence their discussion."[48] It's easy to understand why the dominant viewpoint will attract more ideas—groups unconsciously strive towards harmony; and, once a position dominates, it becomes an easy reference point that frames and colors the view of the group members.

So what can a community association manager or board member do to shift the position of the group away from the dominant viewpoint?

The Informational Influence

If a person relies on the power of the informational influence, and provides information to the group, he or she can shift the group position away from the dominant viewpoint. However, how one goes about providing relevant information is very important.

When making statements, people "often entangle information about [their] *arguments* with cues concerning [their] *position* on the issue. But when people hear relevant arguments without learning the specific stands other people assume they still shift their positions. *Arguments*, in and of themselves, matter."[49]

It's important to disentangle one's personal position *on* the issue from arguments *about* the issue. The power of information to sway a group is obviously weakened if that information or argument is little more than a reiteration of a position. When groups are divided on an issue, one side may disagree with the position of the other side, refusing to hear the arguments.

I have experienced this first-hand in my own five-unit association where each of the unit owners is a trustee. As our self-managed association was going through a tortured process of redecorating the common areas (a process that started two years before I moved in), decisions had to be made about wallpaper. As one of the trustees was showing wallpaper samples—and stating that she loved them—another trustee, who obviously delighted in disagreeing with others, immediately responded that it wouldn't work. It's possible that if one trustee had authoritatively stated that, say, stripes or florals were the patterns we were trying to emulate (that is, if she had provided information), it would have been more difficult for the other trustee to disagree—unless she too had information, rather than statements about likes or dislikes, to support her choice.

During my research I observed a situation that is a perfect illustration of the need for a strong and impassioned argument:

A condominium association was undergoing extensive renovations on both the exterior and interior of the building, so the seven-member board decided to form a decorating committee. It was the first committee the association had ever empowered—other than a social committee that was responsible for occasional parties. (My most charitable assessment of this community's committee structure is that it was severely anemic.) So, under the circumstances, a decorating committee was a very good idea; and, in fact, there was great enthusiasm for the idea.

Remarkably, though, the board promptly assigned three of the five seats on the decorating committee to—themselves! Of these three, one was the

---

Putting the Informational Influence to Work

There are a few techniques for using the informational influence effectively. They include:

Quote the experts: When you make definitive statements referring to authoritative sources (like research publications) you create a distance between your personal position on an issue and the argument for or against the issue itself because such sources represent the views and opinions of third parties. Such statements seem credible and objective. Also, they should be devoid of content that makes them seem emotional.

Use statistics: People are enormously attracted to the power of numbers, even though numbers can be used to mislead. It's what Robert Cialdini calls the consensus effect of influence. For instance, we often decide what movie or television program to watch or which book to buy based on which of these is attracting the greatest number of people. That's why *The New York Times* publishes a bestsellers list and why Nielsen ratings are so valuable to television producers and advertisers. We're curious about what attracts others and we're reassured to know that others have made the same choice—it provides a certain sense of comfort.

Be bold: Make an impassioned argument on the issue. Let's face it, most people don't like to engage in public disagreements. Instead, they'll express their ideas mildly and very diplomatically. However, "like inoculations against disease even weak arguments will prompt counterarguments, which are then available for a stronger attack."[50] This is called attitude inoculation. When people are exposed to a series of mild arguments against their position on a given issue, they become entrenched in their position and very adept at brushing off increasingly stronger arguments. Hence, if you want someone to change their position on a key issue, you are much better off presenting an impassioned and strong argument at the very outset. This will give you a greater chance to sway the position of the other side.

---

president and one was very friendly with another board member who was not on the committee. These two friends *always* voted together—which meant that, essentially, four members of the board were on the decorating committee. And, for all practical purposes, the three board members constituted a quorum on the decorating committee thus enabling them to pass any decision they wished. In essence, the decorating committee became more powerful than the association board.

As I observed the board's deliberations, I didn't hear any objections about board members serving on the decorating committee. If anything, the idea was seen in a positive light—it would allow for superb communications between the committee and the board. Informational influences were hard at work in this board's decision-making process, and the pooling of ideas clearly favored the dominant viewpoint.

As for the mandate of the decorating committee, the board gave the committee no specific instructions on the budget nor an idea of the scope of the interior decoration project. There was a general sense that the walls needed repainting, the hallway carpets definitely needed to be replaced, and the decorating committee would select an acceptable color palette.

The association had about $180,000 in reserves, and although that is a sizable amount, it wouldn't cover replacing a second elevator that didn't run or repairing major structural problems in the building.

For about six months the decorating committee worked very hard, sometimes meeting twice a week. They hired—and soon fired—an interior decorator, at a cost of $15,000 to the association. The board downplayed the loss, choosing to view it philosophically and to appreciate how many hours of work the committee had put in. During this time, the committee made no reports to the board (except for the interior decorator fiasco), although they did assure the board that their work was going well and they were making progress. Eventually, the committee hired another interior decorator, and at the end of the six months announced that the decorator would make a presentation to the owners and residents.

A day before the presentation, the association president (and decorating committee member) left a rather long message on each board member's answering machine. He asked everyone to be tolerant and to accept all the recommendations of the committee because they had worked so hard and spent so many hours on the project that they needed to be respected for their hard work and needed to feel empowered. This implied that dissent amounted to disrespect.

Twelve people attended the decorator's presentation—the decorating committee, three of their spouses, and the board.

The proposed scope of work came as a surprise—new drop ceilings, new door handles, new chandeliers, and new sconces. The biggest surprise was the proposal to tear up the foyer's marble floor and replace it with wall-to-wall carpeting.

As the presentation went on, a board member (who hadn't been on the decorating committee) became increasingly uncomfortable until, finally, she asked whether a final decision had been made about the marble floors. Yes, the decision was final, but neither the decorator nor the committee could tell her how much it would cost.

At this point this board member made a very impassioned argument about the board member's fiduciary responsibility and their accountability.

Until she spoke up, the group polarization had been so pronounced, and the pooling of ideas had so strongly favored the dominant perspective, that none of the decorating committee members had seen that replacing marble floors that were in excellent condition with wall-to-wall carpeting is actually a downgrade and a waste of money. But her impassioned argument broke the bind of the informational influence, and the board decided to get quotes for tearing up the marble floors.

It's clear that arguments do matter, and they constitute the basis of informational influences affecting group polarization. However, the most important factors are knowing how to present an argument without entangling it with the position and being prepared to make a strong and impassioned argument to mitigate the effects of group polarization.

Normative Influences

Normative influence is the other major factor contributing to group polarization. "According to normative influence, judgment shifts result from exposure to others' choice preferences and subsequent conformity to implicit or explicit norms in these preferences."[51] That is, we're influenced by the positions other people take on specific issues. "As Leon Festinger argued in his influential theory of social comparison, it is human nature to want to evaluate our opinions and abilities, something we can do by comparing our views with those of others. We are most persuaded by people in our 'reference groups'—groups we identify with. Moreover, wanting people to like us, we might express stronger opinions after discovering that others share our views."[52]

Everyone has experienced a group situation with normative influences hard at work. For instance, a group of people who don't know one another very well will begin their conversations with safe topics like the weather and slowly progress into more substantive conversations. Once a person has established a common ground with someone else on a substantive issue, they become more comfortable and begin to open up and express their preferences on the issue.

However, "it's surprising that, instead of simply conforming to the group average, people often go it one better."[53] This may stem from the urge of an individual to "enhance one's position in the group and/or one's self-image, and to verify the adequacy of one's behavior. . . . By being more extreme than the group average, one is presenting oneself as both similar to others and distinctive in the approved direction."[54] For example, at the annual homeowners meeting, after some socializing and small talk around the punch bowl, several young women discover that they all have toddlers about the same age. Having established this common interest, they compare notes and exchange anecdotes. When one mother remarks that her three-year-old is beginning to read, she becomes the focus of the group.

Normative influences explain why sometimes groups become obsessed with particular issues. When this happens, the group often fails to consider valuable alternative solutions.

Word-of-mouth advertising is a good illustration of the power of normative influences at work. It's well known that this is one of the most effective ways to advertise. Consider, for example, when community associations decide to use certain products or contractors because other associations, or reference groups, have used them. Such testimony and reference to practices used by others amounts to word-of-mouth advertising. Indeed, community association managers use this technique when recommending a certain course of action to a client.

And, of course, informational and normative influences can and do work simultaneously—for instance, as mentioned above, when people buy a book because it's on the bestseller list or see a movie because it won an Academy Award.

Minority Influence

What should you do if your opinion is the minority opinion *and* it's unpopular?

Through his research Serge Moscovici has "identified several determinants of minority influence: consistency, self-confidence, and defections from the majority."[55]

Consistency

Minority positions must remain consistent if they are to prevail. Granted, this is a tough proposition that has caused much pain for adherents of minority views. David Myers advises those holding minority views to "prepare yourself for ridicule, especially when you argue an issue that's personally relevant to the majority and when the group wants to settle an issue by reaching consensus."[56]

Labels are common expressions of ridicule. Troublemaker, tightwad, stupid, loudmouth, crazy—these are the labels we put on people in our communities who don't agree with our thinking.

Self-Confidence

Culturally, we value self-confidence immensely. We know, for instance, that self-confidence is one of the key factors in communicating expertise.

Proponents of a minority position will enhance that position in the group if they display self-confidence. Indeed, displaying or expressing self-confidence will shatter the confidence of the group's majority. In fact, research has shown that "any behavior by a minority that conveys self-confidence, such as taking the head seat at the table, tends to raise self-doubts among the majority."[57]

Consistent and Confident

Ultimately, it's "a persistent minority [that] punctures any illusion of unanimity. When a minority consistently doubts the majority wisdom, majority mem-

---

Brainstorming Rules

- **No criticizing.** Reserve judgment until later.
- **Be wild and free.** It's easier to tame down than think up.
- **Be prolific.** The more ideas, the better the chance of finding a good one.
- **Combine and improve.** Mix and match everyone's ideas.

---

bers become freer to express their own doubts and might even switch to the minority position."[58] Indeed, history has progressed because people defected from the majority position to the minority position until the minority became a majority and a new minority emerged.

Brainstorming

Brainstorming is a popular technique for generating ideas in groups. Alex Osborn came up with the concept about 45 years ago. He found it useful for the work of his advertising agency.[59] Osborn's brainstorming technique relies on four basic rules:

"Criticism is ruled out. Adverse judgments of ideas must be withheld until later.

"'Free-wheeling' is welcome. The wilder the idea the better; it is easier to tame down than to think up.

"Quantity is wanted. The greater the number of ideas, the more the likelihood of winners.

"Combination and improvement are sought. In addition to contributing ideas of their own, participants should suggest how ideas of others can be turned into *better* ideas, or how two or more ideas can be joined into still another idea."[60]

What Makes Brainstorming Succeed?

First, participants need to feel uninhibited. Osborn's rules attempt to create a safe environment for people to express their ideas. This is important because the process won't be successful if people feel inhibited.

Second, participants need to separate their contributions to the brainstorming session from their personal self worth. Some people will get too attached to their own ideas and will be hurt when the group doesn't use them. So participants need to understand that, in this process, any and all the ideas may ultimately be turned down.

Third, the group needs to start with a well-formulated question or a clearly defined problem. "Uninhibited creativity combined with ambiguity can produce a general sense of confusion."[61]

What Makes Brainstorming Fail?

Despite the popularity of brainstorming, research has shown that it may not be as effective as we think. Experiments have demonstrated that groups of people working *individually* generate more ideas than groups of people working *together*. There are two possible explanations for this.

First, the pooling of ideas (even during brainstorming) might start favoring the dominant perspective, or the group may become polarized.

Second, some people won't participate—at least not up to their potential. This is called social loafing, a "tendency for people to exert less effort when they pool their efforts toward a common goal than when they are individually accountable."[62]

When people aren't individually accountable for what the group accomplishes, social loafing increases. My daughter Susan complains when she's given a group assignment at school because the teacher gives the same grade to each member of the group without taking into account the students' individual contributions.

We see this in community associations as well. Unless one member of the board is directly accountable for a particular outcome, the same questions will remain on the table month after month without any progress. Assigning individual accountability will unquestionably raise the overall effectiveness of the group.

CHAPTER 4

Groupthink

Do groups of highly educated, intelligent, and empowered people make better decisions than ordinary citizens from all walks of life, such as community association board members, who may or may not have the privilege of a stellar education or a high-powered job? Does a good education coupled with high social position protect an individual from the influences of a small group setting? Not necessarily. If anything, some of the world's worst and most disastrous decisions have been made by groups of nation-state presidents and their advisors. Irving Janis argues that "the members of policy-making groups, no matter how mindful they may be of their exalted national status and of their heavy responsibilities, are subjected to the pressures widely observed in groups of ordinary citizens."[63]

Studying decision making in groups of leaders who are making decisions of national importance is very useful because it enables us to understand better how group dynamics influence decision making. Indeed, psychologist Irving Janis was motivated to learn to what extent groups of well-educated and high-powered decision makers were susceptible to the influences of group dynamics. He summarized his findings in two very influential books (*Victims of Groupthink*, published in 1972 and *Groupthink*, published in 1982) in which he explained how groups of highly empowered individuals could reach bad decisions through a flawed decision-making process.

Group Cohesion

Small groups that meet on a regular basis are typically cohesive groups. In general, group cohesion is viewed as "the overall strength of positive relationships within the group. Groups can be cohesive for a variety of reasons. Indeed, cohesion has been defined as the sum of all pressures acting to keep individuals in a group."[64] Cohesive groups may result from the simple affection of the group members toward each other, or their drive to achieve a goal that may only be possible through membership in the group. Also, group membership may be associated with certain status, may provide a sense of identity, and may be a rewarding experience in and of itself. Above all, group cohesion breeds loyalty, commitment, and even sacrifice among the group members.[65]

For some individuals service on their community association's board has become part of their identity. Their position on the association board is so important that they may even include it on their resume as proof of accomplishments and leadership skills. I once met a woman who had been on her association's board for more than 26 years, and who thought of herself as the "mommy" of the association—to use her words. Also, retired individuals or stay-at-home parents may turn to board activism to channel their energies. We may complain of association members' apathy, and want to encourage this kind of activism, but we should also be aware that a group that becomes too cohesive may be a problem for the association if its decisions become focused primarily on maintaining the group's cohesion.

Overall, while group cohesiveness may seem like a positive phenomenon it inevitably leads to certain pressures within the group. "In all [cohesive] groups…members tend to evolve informal norms to preserve friendly intra-group relations and these become part of the hidden agenda of their meetings."[66] This "hidden agenda" may turn into a mission to preserve the group, even at the expense of good decisions. In the end, loyalty to the group is highly valued in cohesive groups.

For his research, Janis studied major events in the recent history of the United States where disastrous decisions were made—America's failure to prevent the bombing of Pearl Harbor, the Bay of Pigs invasion orchestrated by the Kennedy Administration, the escalation of the Vietnam War during the Johnson Administration, and the Watergate cover up by the Nixon Administration. These cases are helpful because of the perspective they provide—if American presidents and their advisers are susceptible to the effects of group dynamics, then we shouldn't be surprised that community association boards are susceptible also.

Groups of powerful individuals, and, for that matter, all small groups, are not doomed to make bad decisions at all times. In fact, small groups are well-equipped to make very good decisions if the symptoms of groupthink are kept in check, and Janis cites the Cuban Missile Crisis and the Marshall Plan as examples of good decisions produced by small groups of very powerful individuals.

What is Groupthink?

Irving Janis coined the term "groupthink" in the spirit of George Orwell's words "doublethink" and "crimethink" which Orwell used in 1984. The central features of groupthink appear as "signs of high cohesiveness and an accompanying concurrence-seeking tendency that interfere with critical thinking."[67] In Janis's own words, "The term 'groupthink' [is] a quick and easy way to refer to a mode of thinking that people engage in when they are deeply involved in a cohesive in-group, when the members' strivings for unanimity override their motivation to realistically appraise alternative courses of action."[68] Janis argues that "groupthink" as a term takes "an invidious connotation. The invidiousness is intentional: Groupthink refers to a deterioration of mental efficiency, reality testing, and moral judgment that results from in-group pressures."[69]

While the scope of this book does not allow a detailed analysis of the case studies used by Janis, it is important to examine the similarities in those cases that led to bad decisions.

Each of the historical cases of bad decision making listed above have two things in common:

1. The decision-making group was cohesive.
2. The decision making was extremely defective.[70]

These two commonalities are concurrence-seeking tendencies, and they increase the danger of decision making resulting in groupthink. Their effect is magnified and more likely to produce symptoms of groupthink when coupled with certain structural features of the group and situational (context) factors. These "play a crucial role in determining whether a moderately or highly cohesive group will develop symptoms of groupthink."[71]

Structural Features That Lead to Groupthink

There are four structural features, or faults, that lead to groupthink,[72] and, frankly, each can be found in community associations:

1. The Group Is Insulated

Homeowner and resident apathy is a reality in many community associations. When the association seems to be humming along fairly well, board members may find themselves becoming isolated. This may be just their perception, but if they also have a sense that others don't care and are not interested in association matters, the board may begin to feel a sense of entitlement or omnipotence. All of this will increase the possibility that their decision making will lead to groupthink.

2. The Group Lacks Impartial Leadership

In one community association a board member had been on the association board since 1974 when the condominium conversion had occurred. I think deep down this woman felt that she was the mother of the association. Her continued presence on the board for nearly 30 years, coupled with her emotional decision-making style, made impartial decisions a rarity.

3. The Group Lacks Procedures

Although the association mentioned above had established procedures for conducting business, they were often circumvented. For example, this board member once hired a superintendent without giving the board an opportunity to examine other candidates. Her unilateral action was based on the fact that she had been able "to relate to this guy" and because he liked the soup that she had so kindly offered him on a cold winter day.

4. The Group Is Homogeneous

It's common knowledge that we are attracted to people who think like we do. Hence, it's easy for a community association board to turn into a homogeneous forum of friends with common views and interests. The homogeneity of the group is almost never achieved as a result of a deliberate conspiracy. Instead, it's usually a slow and insidious process. People tend to invite others to join the board in their association whom they like and tend to agree with on a score of issues.

Group Situations That Lead to Groupthink

For a cohesive group of decision makers to exhibit symptoms of groupthink, a situation must also occur that, in many ways, reflects the psychological factors affecting the group. Janis identified two situations that lead to symptoms of groupthink:

1. High stress from external threats with a low hope of a better solution from the leaders.
2. Low self-esteem temporarily induced by:
   ■ Recent failures that make members' inadequacies salient
   ■ Excessive difficulties on current decision-making tasks that lower each member's sense of self-efficacy
   ■ Moral dilemmas: apparent lack of feasible alternatives except those that violate ethical standards.[73]

For many people, who identify first with their families and second with their jobs or religious and civic interests, serving on the association board may be a tertiary responsibility. They may transfer a lot of their stress and pressure into the process of decision-making on their community association's board.

Groups' concurrence-seeking tendencies, combined with organizational structural patterns and the psychological factors that lead to groupthink "might be best understood as a mutual effort among the members of the group to maintain emotional equanimity in the face of external and internal sources of stress arising when they share responsibility for making vital decisions that pose threats of failure, social disapproval and self-disapproval. The eight symptoms of groupthink form a coherent pattern if viewed in the context of this explanatory hypothesis. The symptoms may function in somewhat different ways to produce the same result."[74]

The Eight Symptoms of Groupthink

In order to avoid groupthink, it's very important to learn to recognize the eight symptoms of groupthink identified by Irving Janis. He divided these eight symptoms into three major types that are familiar features of many (although not all) cohesive groups.

Type 1. The group overestimates its power and morality.

Symptom 1. The group has "An illusion of invulnerability, shared by most or all the members, which creates excessive optimism and encourages taking extreme risks."[75]

This primary symptom of groupthink shows itself in at least two ways. First, group members may become excessively optimistic either about their power or about their leader's power. Second, they may ignore warnings about the pitfalls of a course of action because they feel invulnerable.[76] For instance, when news broke that there was a connection between the Watergate break in and White House personnel, members of Nixon's inner circle were overconfident about their ability to deal with a troublesome situation. Post-Watergate research and interviews with Nixon's inner circle have shown that throughout the months of the investigation they did not consider criminal punishment, impeachment, or resignation even a remote possibility. History showed that their sense of invulnerability was unfounded.[77]

Symptom 2. The group has "An unquestioned belief in the group's inherent morality, inclining the members to ignore the ethical or moral consequences of their decisions."[78]

This symptom of groupthink was obvious in the meetings of Lyndon Johnson's inner circle dubbed the Tuesday Lunch Group. The decisions made by this group defined America's policy during the war in Vietnam. It's possible that, as this group first formed, members had differing attitudes about the evils of communism and America's role in Vietnam.

However, it's been argued that, "the few members [of the group] who had spent many years participating in military planning conferences at the Pentagon may have introduced to the rest of the group a detached, dehumanizing attitude toward the Vietnam War, using euphemistic vocabulary such as 'body counts,' 'surgical air strikes,' and 'pacification.' "[79] This may have softened the thinking of those opposed to the war, enabling them to ignore the grave moral and ethical consequences of their decisions. In essence, this vocabulary of dehumanization may have created the false impression that America's engagement in Vietnam was not an ethical or moral compromise, but rather was the act of a savior.

In community conflicts, opposing groups and individuals also embrace this symptom of groupthink. They will see the other side in negative or dismissive terms and minimize the possible moral and ethical consequences of their decisions. In these situations, people rationalize their behavior by believing the other side is at fault and deserved the negative outcome. The potency of negative labels has been recognized by CAI, and as a result, CAI's Board of Trustees, in conjunction with CAI Research Foundation's Board of Directors, have recently focused their energies on developing a

"Unquestioned belief in the inherent morality"—of the board.

I was invited to observe the board meeting of a rather sizable community association that was in the initial stages of a serious conflict.

The board had just imposed a major assessment on its 300 units to upgrade each of their 300 garage doors. The problem was that only about 80 of the garage doors had problems, while the other 220 had none. Most residents whose garage doors were not affected felt strongly that the assessment was a waste of money and could be avoided by replacing only the faulty garage doors.

The board, however, reasoned otherwise. They argued that the existing doors were a constant financial drain in terms of repairs and did not justify further investment. Since the bylaws of the association mandated that all garage doors be uniform and manufactured by the same company, the board felt compelled to replace all the doors, including the overwhelming majority of the doors that worked just fine.

At one point during the meeting, the association's president whispered in my ear, "I have one of those 80 malfunctioning doors." Then he added with a smile, "I want the nicer upgrade model, so, we're going to get it." While I appreciated his off-the-record honesty and sincerity, I didn't fully understand why replacing all the doors was such a splendid idea, even though I had been brought in to advise the board how to avoid a major community conflict over the assessment.

Many association members at this meeting asked what seemed to be rather reasonable questions, and after the meeting the board members discussed what had transpired. They informed me, almost in unison, that the first gentleman who had asked questions about the assessment was crazy. The next woman who spoke was said to be a constant troublemaker. They had a characterization for each resident who asked questions.

Clearly, I was observing a groupthink symptom. This group had no doubts about the inherent morality of their decisions; and, hence, they were rather unconcerned about possible moral or ethical consequences imposed on the "crazies," and "troublemakers." These words—just like "body count" and "surgical air strikes"—created a safe distance between "us" and "them," which, in turn, led to the justification and rationalization of their decisions. —jm new, more friendly and benevolent lexicon that will be more conducive to promoting harmony in communities.

Type 2. The group is closed minded.

Symptom 3. "Collective efforts to rationalize in order to discount warning or other information that might lead the members to reconsider their assumptions before they recommit themselves to their past policy decisions."[80] In other words, the group comes up with excuses for, or arguments that dismiss, information that might make them rethink a decision.

This symptom of groupthink was evident in President Johnson's Tuesday Lunch Group's decisions regarding the war in Vietnam. It's well known that the war in Vietnam evolved as a series of decisions escalated America's involvement in the war, and the Tuesday Lunch Group was primarily responsible for those decisions.

The Tuesday Lunch Group was fully committed to the idea that if Vietnam bowed to communist rule, all the Asian nations would fall—like dominos—to the communists. In the very least, this theory represented a gross oversimplification without taking into account the socio-political and cultural realities in various Asian nations.

However, having internalized the domino theory, the Tuesday Lunch Group—which was by its nature a highly cohesive group—felt compelled to make decisions that wouldn't counter their initial determinations. In cohesive groups, "as [it] often happens, the members feel that loyalty to the group requires unwavering support of the group's past policy decisions, [and] the usual psychological tendency to bolster past commitments is reinforced."[81]

This very same dynamic can occur on community association boards. A board may, for instance, be so committed to maintaining architectural control that allowing a variance for a specific case may be seen as the beginning of the entire association going down the drain.

Sometimes the group of community association decision makers becomes so deeply mired in their commitment to past decisions that they may act in ways that are detrimental to the well-being of the entire association. Gary Caufield, an attorney specializing in community association law, told me that he once represented a woman who was suffering from severe asthma. Doctors had advised this woman that she should live in a house with central air conditioning. She first approached the association board of her 10-unit building requesting that the association allow her to install central air conditioning in her unit. Since the infrastructure necessary for such an arrangement would have to deal with some common area elements, the board turned her down.

According to Gary, his client loved her unit so much that she was willing to spend about $150,000 of her own money to install central air conditioning in everyone's units. His client had both engineering and architectural reports attesting that it was possible to install central air conditioning in the entire building and that there would be no unsightly structures in common areas afterward. In addition to getting the convenience of central air conditioning, the value of all the units in the building would increase significantly. Gary Caufield and his client expected the request to be green-lighted without a hitch. To their surprise, however, the board decided that they wouldn't depart from their original decision. While this board's decision didn't have the consequences that the Tuesday Lunch Group's decisions had, their logic, or, rather, illogic, is the same.

Symptom 4. The group holds "Stereotyped views of enemy leaders as too evil to warrant genuine attempts to negotiate, or as too weak and stupid to counter whatever risky attempts are made to defeat their purposes."[82]

Such a stereotyped view of the opponent was evident in the decisions that led to the Bay of Pigs fiasco. Arthur Schlesinger later explained that, "Castro was regarded as a weak 'hysteric' leader whose army was ready to defect; he was considered so stupid that 'although warned by air strikes, he would do nothing to neutralize the Cuban underground.' This is a stunning example of the classical stereotype of the enemy as weak and ineffectual."[83]

Likewise, in the course of decision making leading to the Korean Conflict, President Truman's advisors viewed communist China as a weak nation largely dependent on the Soviet Union, both in terms of domestic and foreign policies. Consequently, they underestimated China's ability to react to the U.S.'s military involvement in Korea. President Truman's advisory group's "failure to scrutinize their stereotyped misconception and to consider alternative hypotheses concerning Red China's capabilities and intentions is a prime symptom of groupthink."[84]

Such stereotyped views of the opponent also occur in community association settings when, for instance, the community is polarized regarding a specific issue. In general, each side tends to view the other as evil, stupid, weak, uncaring, or troublesome.

This stereotyped view is the reason people break up into in-groups and out-groups. The "we" in the in-group are viewed as kind, smart, nice, strong, law-abiding individuals, whereas the "they" of the out-group are seen as evil, stupid, unpleasant, weak, outlaws.

Type 3. The group is pressured to be uniform

Symptom 5. Group members engage in, "Self-censorship of deviations from the apparent group consensus, reflecting each member's inclination to minimize to himself the importance of his doubts and counterarguments."[85] Or in other words, people tend to stop themselves from going against the group by saying to themselves: my concerns aren't important, my contrary and dissenting ideas aren't worth mentioning.

Enemies Too Weak, Stupid, or Evil to Deal With—Living Right in Your Association

Carrie Martoni tells a story that demonstrates the dynamic of stereotyping and consequently underestimating the "other" in a community association.

Carrie bought a house in a community association in suburban Boston that allowed only white blinds and curtains. Carrie, like many new community association members, didn't read all the rules and regulations prior to purchase. When she moved in she installed red blinds in a third-floor window—which immediately had the board seeing red!

The opening volley in this conflict came in the form of a letter from the board in which Carrie learned that she had broken a rule and which demanded that she remove the red blinds immediately. The letter was rude and implied that Carrie was an uncaring member of the community and that she was stupid to flout the association's rules.

In her interview she told me that she would have been more cooperative about removing the blinds had she first been approached politely.

Carrie's assessment that she was viewed as stupid by the board was confirmed when she overheard one of the board members while conducting a tour of the association. The board member pointed to the grounds and walkways of Carrie's front yard—which had bricks set in cement rather than customary sand—and said, "See, I told you she's stupid. If she weren't stupid she wouldn't have paid to have the bricks set in cement." Carrie says that she opened the door and yelled out, "I am neither stupid nor cheap—that's why my bricks are set in cement."

Carrie and her association ended up in a Massachusetts court, and each spent a lot of time and money. "If they only hadn't insulted me in the beginning," said Carrie, "I would have certainly been more cooperative." —jm

Self-censorship was very much a factor in Nixon's inner circle as the Watergate scandal was unfolding. The group felt so invulnerable that even Nixon thought of the scandal merely as a public relations problem. "I felt sure," he said in retrospect, "that it was just a public relations problem that only needed a public relations solution."[86]

Understandably, such an underestimation of the gravity of the situation made all the group members susceptible to the "contagious effect of the optimism exuded by the leader."[87] This optimism created pressures within the group to suppress any impulses to the contrary, thus, resulting in self-censorship. For instance, John Dean—who along with inner-circle members Haldeman, Ehrlichman, and Colson contributed to the decisions that led to the Watergate scandal—provides a good example of self-censorship within the group. "Despite his mounting misgivings, Dean apparently was caught up in the group atmosphere of high optimism, sufficiently so that time and again he conveyed a rosy picture to the others."[88] A few weeks later Dean became aware that the cover-up would not work and that something urgently needed to be done if they were to avoid criminal charges. In a March 21, 1973, meeting with Nixon he called for urgent action. Nixon was aware of the new developments, but when he "raised skeptical questions, Dean reverted to his habitual compliant response, 'to snap to my usual optimism for his benefit.' "[89] Clearly, by "snapping to his usual optimism" John Dean censored himself.

Granted, I have a hard time thinking of any act of self-censorship on any community association board that could possibly have the gravity of the Watergate scandal. Yet how many times has self-censorship resulted in bad board decisions? The sad answer is: many. Indeed, community association board members often tell me how they, too, have silently acquiesced to a bad decision—they had their misgivings, or at least a gnawing thought in the back of their heads telling them that something wasn't right. Yet they censored themselves, thus making this symptom of groupthink a reality.

Symptom 6. The group has "A shared illusion of unanimity concerning judgments conforming to the majority view (partly resulting from self-censorship of deviations, augmented by the false assumption that silence means consent)."[90] In other words, each member of the group thinks that everyone else agrees with the decision.

In essence, this is a pressure towards unanimity within the group. Indeed, most groups that succumb to groupthink have a heightened sense of internal cohesion and strive for unanimity in all of their decisions. Departure from a unanimous decision can be viewed as a threat to the integrity of the group itself.

For instance, *The Pentagon Papers* and interviews with President Johnson's Tuesday Lunch Group show that maintaining unanimity was one of their central goals. Even those who had reservations about certain tactics used in Vietnam took special pains to affirm their commitment to the Tuesday Lunch Group's strategic approaches.[91] The need for unanimity thus effectively suppressed any form of meaningful dissent.

I have observed this pull towards unanimity on many community association boards. In fact, some boards arrive, unconsciously, at the conclusion that unanimity on the board equals peace and harmony in the association. Dissent on the board is viewed as destructive and demoralizing. This, unfortunately, in the long run, may put the association at peril because suppressing dissent for the sake of unanimity may lead to bad decisions, just as it happened in the case of the war in Vietnam.

Symptom 7. The group places "Direct pressure on any member that expresses strong arguments against any of the group's stereotypes, illusions, or commitments, making clear that this type of dissent is contrary to what is expected of all loyal members."[92]

Defense Secretary Robert McNamara, who was one of the key members of President Johnson's Tuesday Lunch Group, expressed reservations about the group's assumption that the "North Vietnamese could be bombed into coming to the negotiating table."[93] His reasoning was based on certain facts that he presented to a senate investigating committee demonstrating that bombing was ineffective. President Johnson and his inner circle were extremely displeased: Johnson compared McNamara's act to a situation in which a "man [was] trying to sell his house, while one of the sons of the family went to a prospective buyer to point out that there were leaks in the basement."[94] As Janis aptly points out, "this line of thought strongly suggests that in his own mind Johnson regarded his in-group of policy advisers as a family and its leading dissident member as an irresponsible son who was sabotaging the family's interests."[95] Clearly, in such a setting any dissent jeopardizing the group's core beliefs and stereotypes is viewed as disloyalty.

As a consequence of his perceived disloyalty, Robert McNamara was eventually isolated from the group and ultimately fired. Obviously, his ouster would allow the Tuesday Lunch Group to return to the undisturbed comfort of cohesive decision making.

Once again, this very same dynamic often demonstrates itself on community association boards that become very cohesive. While decisions of community association boards usually do not have the far-reaching consequences of decisions reached by a presidential group of advisors, they are nonetheless key to attaining a harmonious community.

Indeed, community association boards make decisions that have important consequences for most people living in the community, if not for the entire community. Board decisions affect important issues such as property rights, resident conduct, and lifestyles. An interesting contradiction arises in that association board members may mistake a sense of cohesion and peace on their board for a sense of well-being for the entire community. Ironically, preserving the sense of peace within the group may result in a shattered sense of peace in the community.

This is exactly what happened when a particularly cohesive community association board decided to remove a large stand of holly trees because they believed the trees might block the view of drivers turning onto the highway from the association. One board member learned from a long-time resident that the trees had been planted many years earlier as a wind break and that removing them would allow the wind to carry sand onto the property from a gravel quarry just below the community. But he elected not to pass the information along to the full board because he knew he would be viewed as a dissenter—the news would be unwelcome, and he would be criticized for delivering it. A little sand wasn't worth upsetting the group's equanimity. Six months later, however, half the community was in an uproar because cars, windows, and other items were being constantly pitted by blowing sand and there was no apparent relief.

Symptom 8. The group experiences "The emergence of self-appointed mind guards—members who protect the group from adverse information that might shatter their shared competency about the effectiveness and morality of their decisions."[96]

For instance, during the decision making that led to the Bay of Pigs fiasco, President Kennedy's adviser, Arthur Schlesinger, was uneasy about invading Cuba. Janis tells us of an incident when Robert Kennedy pulled Schlesinger aside at a birthday party and told him, "You may be right or you may be wrong, but the President has made up his mind. Don't push it any further. Now is the time for everyone to help him all they can."[97] In Janis's opinion, in this conversation Robert Kennedy acted as a "mind guard."

Irving Janis argues that "Just as a bodyguard protects the President and other high officials from injurious physical assaults, a mind guard protects them from thoughts that might damage their confidence in the soundness of the policies to which they are committed or to which they are about to commit themselves."[98]

You may have encountered mind guards at work or in your community. Mind guards are usually very dedicated to the leader of the organization. It's also possible that since they enjoy their proximity to the leader, protecting the leader and the leader's decisions also protects themselves. Others can also perceive a mind guard's behavior as lobbying for a specific position.

We can see that the symptoms of groupthink are very real, very potent, and very obvious in the decision making of groups of ordinary people as well as presidential advisors. However, what's most important is to understand that these symptoms of groupthink lead to defective decision making.

CHAPTER 5

The Seven Major Defects of Group Decision Making

Irving Janis identified seven major defects that contribute to a small group's inability to make decisions that lead to good outcomes or produce adequate solutions to problems:

1. The group's discussions are limited to a few alternative courses of action (often only two) without a survey of the full range of alternatives.

2. The group does not survey the objectives to be fulfilled and the values implicated by the choice.

3. The group fails to reexamine the course of action initially preferred by the majority from the standpoint of non-obvious risks and drawbacks that had not been considered when it was originally evaluated.

4. The group neglects courses of action initially evaluated as unsatisfactory by the majority. They spend little or no time discussing whether they have overlooked non-obvious gains or whether there are ways of reducing the seemingly prohibitive costs that have made the alternatives seem undesirable.

5. The members make little or no attempt to obtain information from experts who can supply sound estimates of losses and gains from alternative courses of action.

6. The group shows selective bias toward facts and relevant judgments from experts, the media, and outside critics: They're interested in facts and opinions that support the policy they preferred initially and spend their meeting time discussing them; but they tend to ignore facts and opinions that do not support the policy they preferred initially.

7. The group spends little time deliberating how the chosen policy might be hindered by bureaucratic inertia, sabotaged by political opponents, or temporarily derailed by the common accidents that happen to the best of well-laid plans. Consequently, they fail to work out contingency plans to cope

with foreseeable setbacks that could endanger the overall success of the chosen course of action.[99]

What these seven defects have in common is that they all produce concurrence-seeking tendencies on the part of the group members. If you recall from our earlier discussion, concurrence-seeking tendencies can be an expression of normative influences leading to group polarization. Quite naturally, most people want peace, comfort, and satisfaction in their working relationships with other members of their small group. Clearly, these are all good and noble intentions. However, these very same good intentions at some point begin to become associated with the mission of the group, leading to an unconscious decision on the part of the group members to protect the group at all costs, often at the expense of their decisions. Under such circumstances, concurrence as a tool of choice becomes a weapon of destruction.

All of the seven major defects contributing to bad decision-making outcomes take place in both our workplaces and on community association boards. I'm sure that if you analyze some of the bad decisions you may have witnessed, or even been part of, you might recall that the group most likely considered very few courses of action. They may not even have come close to considering alternatives that might have resulted in good outcomes. Then, just as we saw in the case of group polarization, the pooling of ideas that follows supports the few alternatives on the table and favors the dominant perspective. Hence, whatever the perspective, it further cements the decision-making strategies of the group.

How to Avoid Decision-Making Defects
Irving Janis recommended nine prescriptions to counter the major defects of small group decision making.

Prescription 1: "The leader of a policy-forming group should assign the role of critical evaluator to each member, encouraging the group to give high priority to airing objectives and doubts. This practice needs to be reinforced by the leader's acceptance of criticism of his or her judgments in order to discourage the members from soft-pedaling their disagreements."[100]

A community association board would have to build a culture of constructive criticism in order to implement this prescription, and the implementation style would be very important. The leader and each member of the group must be aware at all times that criticism should be directed toward issues—not the people articulating them.

Group members must avoid the tendency to equate a person's views on a single issue with the general outlook and personality of that individual. When adopting this prescription, limit the time for criticism. Encourage people to express their views succinctly without wasting the group's time.

Prescription 2: "The leaders in an organization's hierarchy, when assigning a policy-planning mission to a group, should be impartial instead of stating preferences and expectations at the outset. This practice requires each leader to limit his or her briefings to unbiased statements about the scope of the problem and the limitations of available resources, without advocating specific proposals he or she would like to see adopted. This allows the conferees the opportunity to develop an atmosphere of open inquiry and to explore impartially a wide range of policy alternatives."[101]

In following this prescription it is helpful to remember the discussion about informational influences provided earlier. The key is to avoid entangling one's position on an issue with information about the issue.

Popular culture provides a helpful example for the application of this prescription. Since the summer of 1999, American television audiences have been attracted to *Who Wants to Be a Millionaire? Millionaire's* example is instructive in that contestants are better off not revealing their inclination when they "Ask the Audience" for help answering a question because they may taint the audience's response. In the same way, when group members learn the specific inclinations of their leader, they may be unconsciously influenced to produce policies duplicating their leader's perceived or real preferences. The more autocratic the leader, the more pronounced this effect will be.

The phenomenon known as confirmation bias may also be at work here. Confirmation bias is a "tendency to search for information that confirms one's preconceptions."[102] We are very susceptible to the influences of authority, and if the views of the leader turn out to be somewhat in line with our preconceptions, we might limit our thinking and more easily affirm the leader's position.

Prescription 3: "The organization should routinely follow the administrative practice of setting up several independent policy-planning and evaluation groups to work on the same policy question, each carrying out its deliberations under a different leader."[103]

While the average community association may not have the resources to do this, they can use committees to come close to this prescription. For this strategy to work well in a community association, it's important that there be no overlap between the board members and the committee members. Remember the story I shared earlier where three members of the board sat on the decorating committee allowing the committee, in essence, to usurp the board functions? That outcome could have been easily avoided if there had been no overlap in committee and board membership.

Prescription 4: "Throughout the period when the feasibility and effectiveness of policy alternatives are being surveyed, the policy-making group should from time to time divide into two or more subgroups to meet separately, under different chairpersons, and then come together to hammer out their differences."[104]

This strategy is important because people often feel freer to express their genuine thoughts in small subgroups than they do in the larger group. The intimacy of a smaller subgroup may allow some individuals to air a dissenting view without threatening the cohesiveness of the group in general. However, it's important to rotate people in the subgroups. This prevents the group from fragmenting into small, potentially antagonistic factions—which might have disastrous consequences for the group in general.

Prescription 5: "Each member of the policy-making group should discuss periodically the group's deliberations with trusted associates in his or her own unit of the organization and report back their reactions."[105]

For community associations this prescription is a simple matter of board members proactively sharing information with other members of the community. Such open exchanges might have a double benefit: first, they would enable association board members to get feedback and ideas from association members that might differ from their original perspective; second, other members of the community, who ordinarily might have been apathetic, may become interested and energized enough to take a more active role in community life and association governance.

Prescription 6: "One or more outside experts or qualified colleagues within the organization who are not core members of the policy-making group should be invited to each meeting on a staggered basis and should be encouraged to challenge the views of the core members."[106]

Community association managers are uniquely qualified to fill this role. First, managers who have earned their credentials are indeed experts on community association issues, and they should be open and willing to share their expertise with the boards that they're working with. Some community association managers might hesitate to contradict a board member or point out the flaws in a board's decision making for fear of alienating or antagonizing them. However, boards retain managers for their expertise, and they can use a variety of tactics to share that expertise without fear. For instance, citing examples of how other associations may have handled similar situations, citing third-party sources, or diplomatically pointing out flaws in the decision-making process without entangling their argument with their personal position are all effective techniques.

Our society has great respect for the opinion of experts. Social psychology defines an expert as someone who combines confidence with knowledge and is willing to communicate their message to the audience.[107] If the community association manager asserts his or her position as an expert, they will likely avoid alienating and antagonizing board members in the process of sharing expertise or even providing constructive criticism. Also, if the community association manager is perceived as an expert, the board may feel like they're getting added value for their money.

Community Association Management Experts Speak Up

During a presentation I made at a CAI conference in Anaheim, California, a community association manager asked me, "So how do we let them know that we're an expert?" My answer, "By saying so, in the first place." Keep in mind that many people may have the same knowledge, but they will not be perceived as an expert unless they are willing to show confidence and communicate their expertise. —jm

Prescription 7: "At every meeting devoted to evaluating policy alternatives, at least one member should be assigned the role of devil's advocate."[108]

This is a useful tactic, especially if the group is unable to attract the participation of an expert, as suggested in Prescription 6. It might be a good idea to rotate this position by assigning the role to a different person at each meeting. If the group is unwilling to follow this prescription, they can make it a rule to consider at least 3–5 options, and as many facets to each of the options.

Prescription 8: "Whenever the policy issue involves relations with a rival nation or organization, a sizable block of time (perhaps an entire session) should be spent surveying all warning signals from the rivals and constructing alternative scenarios of the rivals' intentions."[109] While I have a hard time imagining a community consumed in neighborly relations or entangled in a dispute with a rival nation, community associations work with organizations, whether rival or friendly on many different levels. Often future disputes can be avoided if the association's board spends time figuring out how to structure their relationship or even how to approach their disputes with other organizations.

I remember a case of a condominium association that had a restaurant in the basement of the building. The restaurant had asked the association for permission to install equipment on a porch roof, and the board granted the request without much deliberation. A few years later, the aging equipment started vibrating and making noise, but since it was grandfathered, not much could be done. The case languished in the courts for years, drained resources and emotions, and resulted in a quagmire. This hardship could have been avoided if the original board had given more attention to their decision to enter into a relationship with another organization.

Another association had better luck in a relationship with a commercial developer by following Prescription 8. This condominium association was located adjacent to an aging shopping center but was also surrounded by lush woods. The association was eager to have the shopping center renovated, but was determined to preserve their pastoral environment as well. When a developer bought the shopping center and announced that he would raze the entire structure and rebuild from scratch, the association formed a committee to scour the newspapers, check county records, and surf the web to monitor the developer's activities and plans. The committee and board were well prepared at each step to protect their interests. After the developer's plans were turned down twice by the county because of the association's well-prepared protests, the developer invited association representatives to participate in the planning and development process. When the project was completed, all the association's interests were protected to the committee's satisfaction; and the developer was so pleased with the final design that he erected a bronze plaque in a central courtyard of the shopping center thanking the members of the association's committee.

Prescription 9: "After reaching a preliminary consensus about what seems to be the best policy alternative, the policy-making group should hold a 'second chance' meeting at which the members are expected to express as vividly as they can all their residual doubts and to rethink the entire issue before making a definitive choice."[110]

This is a very useful prescription in cases of strategic decisions with long-term and far-reaching consequences. Sometimes, taking a break and returning to the issue is a very useful exercise because, if we dwell too much on something, we tend to overlook mistakes or shortcomings that might otherwise seem obvious.

You may have experienced this when writing. When you look at something too much and you're too engrossed in thinking about what you're writing, it's possible to overlook even a glaring mistake. The perspective of time and relative distance from the intense engagement in the task may enable group members to see mistakes that they had missed earlier or to even think of alternatives that they had failed to consider initially.

Oddly, although groups may not routinely follow Prescription 9, on a personal level we use it fairly regularly when we make major decisions. Before getting married or changing jobs, people will gather family and friends and ask them—in one way or another—to express "as vividly as they can all their residual doubts and rethink the entire issue before making a definitive choice."

Satisficing

The decision-making defects within small groups can be reinforced by the group's unconscious desire to satisfice. No, this isn't a spelling mistake. The word "satisfice" is used to refer to public policy-making decisions. While satisficing, "sometimes a decision-maker may simplify a problem of choice by deciding on satisfactory levels for some (but not all) attributes of an outcome."[111] When satisficing occurs, groups identify one or two criteria that are most important to them and focus their attention on meeting those criteria. In this process some other important issues may be overlooked leading to defective decision making.

Satisficing occurs when decision makers are pressured to please multiple constituencies—like community associations. How many times have you said or heard, "Can't please everyone?" However, as soon as decision makers feel they have an alternative that might actually please everyone, they rush to satisfice. So, the standard of pleasing may be simplified by finding the lowest common denominator that everyone might agree to.

While satisficing may sometimes result in good decisions, there's no guarantee of reaching one. Satisficing approaches "simplify some of the exceedingly complex problems one encounters in defining a preference" while making decisions.[112]

Without paying much attention to it, we make many decisions by satisficing. Organizational theorists at Carnegie-Mellon University found that "in practice many decisions are made by choosing the first good alternative that appears. In other words, the decision maker satisfices with respect to all attributes [i.e., criteria of decision making]."[113] As an example they cite the fact that "many families, especially those who are subject to frequent business transfers, buy houses this way. Frequently, it is the most sensible approach, particularly if the costs of delay are high."[114] Unfortunately, deciding where to buy a home through satisficing is how many people become community association members, and this is why they're unaware of and unprepared for many aspects of community association living.

CHAPTER 6

The Power of Persuasion on Groups

I n order to be effective members of groups, we must learn to appreciate the potent powers of persuasion. Whether we like it or not, we spend much of our lives persuading others or being persuaded by others. Persuasion is present in our most mundane tasks—even when we aren't really paying much attention. For instance, before I got to my office today, where I am writing this book, I stopped by the health club to renew my membership. I got a good discount, but I had to argue for it. So, I guess my persuasion worked well. Next I purchased theater tickets, which entailed gently persuading the box office attendant to find the best possible seats. Following this, I stopped by the Boston Public Library to renew a couple of books and pay a fine; and, I made sure that the computer system actually reflected my payment. And, then, I went to the post office for a few routine transactions, one of which was to convince the sales clerk to let me choose from a variety of stamps so I could purchase the ones I liked.

When I finally arrived at my office, I also had to deal with community association issues. I had to phone my association's new management company to explain that their billing did not reflect my prepaid assessment. Then, I had to contact another community association management company, whose plumbers we use, and schedule a service call at our property at a convenient time the next day. Much persuasion had gone on earlier to make this request a possibility because this company's policy is to service only the properties it manages.

These are all very routine, daily transactions for the average person who doesn't necessarily view them as persuading others. However, from the perspective of social psychology, persuasion is at the core of even these mundane tasks.

Advertising, Selling, Persuading

The most obvious form of persuasion is advertising—our modern-day society is surrounded by it. Jean Kilbourne, the acclaimed critic of the advertising industry, estimates that on average we are exposed to 3,000 ads a day.[115] Although this number may initially seem staggering, it isn't if you consider all the ads that appear on billboards, in newspapers, magazines, and even community association bulletins and newsletters. Ads pop up at you on the Internet, glare at you in public places, and even drive by on the sides of buses and trains.

While we view advertising as a function of sales, the connection between sales and persuasion is virtually indistinguishable. Although the word "sales" doesn't show up in every job title or job description, selling is at the core of every job. No matter what our job is, we need to master the power of persuasion to do it efficiently and effectively. We need to sell others on our ideas by being highly persuasive. For instance, when I teach my class, I'm actually selling or persuading—and the product that I'm selling is ideas. As a matter of fact, you, the reader, are involved in and exposed to persuasion right now as you read this book.

Persuasion in Community Associations

Persuasion is a key factor in the life of any organization, including community associations. First, people are persuaded in one way or another to buy into the community association. Then they are persuaded to participate in the life of the community. If they become their community association's board or committee members, they have to persuade others that their policies are worth accepting and implementing. And the various professionals who work with community associations—whether they're community association managers, attorneys, insurance executives, or construction contractors—must constantly persuade their clients to take one action or another. Also, the powers of persuasion define the dynamics within small groups like boards and committees that are at the core of decision making in community associations.

How Persuasion Works

Since persuasion is such an important part of our lives, knowing how it works will help us be more effective in group settings.

While as *homo sapiens* we would like to think of ourselves as creatures who endow every decision with much thought, that isn't necessarily true. Richard Petty, a social psychologist whose expertise focuses on persuasion, argues that "The basic idea is that sometimes people like to and are able to think before they make decisions and sometimes decisions are made without much thought. So we have this continuum of thinking from very high levels of thought where careful deliberation occurs before forming a judgment or decision, which we refer to as the central route, to very little thought, consideration, and elaboration, which we refer to as the peripheral route."[116]

Overall, research shows that "well-educated or analytical people are more responsive to rational appeals than are less educated or less analytical people. Thoughtful, involved audiences travel the central route; they are most responsive to reasoned arguments. Disinterested audiences travel the peripheral route; they are more affected by how much they like the communicator."[117]

The Central Route of Persuasion

The central route of persuasion "views attitude change as resulting from a person's diligent consideration of information that s/he feels is central to the true merits of a particular attitudinal position."[118] In essence, an individual who responds to the central route of persuasion is probably the type of person with highly analytical skills that is focused on the merits of the product. For instance, advertising that uses the central route of persuasion in promoting cellular phones would focus on the monthly cost, the calling radius, and sound quality.

The Peripheral Route of Persuasion

In contrast to the central route of persuasion, when the peripheral route of persuasion is used, "attitude changes do not occur . . . because an individual has personally considered the pros and cons of the issue, but because the attitude issue or object is associated with positive or negative cues—or because the person makes a simple inference about the merits of the advocated position based on various simple cues in the persuasion context."[119] This means that people who respond to the peripheral route of persuasion aren't making decisions based on analytical thinking or criteria, but instead they respond to cues from emotional approaches that appeal to them. For instance, if an ad for cellular phones emphasizes the fact that you can easily change the phone's color to match your moods or clothing, and if the ad also portrays a young, hip, and fashionable lifestyle for those who use such a versatile phone, then we have a clear case where the peripheral route of advertising is being used.

Combining the Central and Peripheral Routes

While the distinction between the central and peripheral routes of advertising is clear, that doesn't mean that the two styles of persuasion function separately. Indeed, most advertising probably combines both forms of persuasion. Even highly-educated people with strong analytical skills aren't immune to the peripheral route of persuasion because it often evokes imagery and positive cues that can sweep almost anyone away.

When it comes to resolving issues and making decisions in a community association, we might assume that association officers would rely on the central route of persuasion. After all, isn't that what fiduciary responsibility is about—making measured, analytical judgments, weighing all the pros and cons objectively, and arriving at sage decisions that will promote the general well-being of the community? Of course, we all know this isn't necessarily the case in real life.

However, it's important to know that from the very beginning of an individual's involvement in the community association, both central and peripheral routes of persuasion are hard at work. Consider the ads for community association properties. They almost always combine both forms of persuasion. For instance, they'll say that the property is fairly priced, conveniently located, and is easily accessible to highways, hospitals and shopping malls (central route arguments). They'll evoke images of idyllic life and instill a sense of problem-free community living (peripheral route arguments).

In order to better understand how the central and peripheral routes of persuasion work, it's important to understand the role that the four elements involved in these routes of persuasion play. These elements are "the communicator, the message, how the message is communicated, and the audience."[120]

The Communicator

Who delivers a message matters to us. In fact, it's impossible to overestimate just how much we're affected by the person delivering the message. For instance, if a resident who has been cast as a troublemaker asks a question about a potential problem during the association's monthly meeting, the question may easily be dismissed. However, if another person, perhaps a new resident, asks the same question it may give rise to serious deliberations resulting in policy-making decisions.

David Myers offers a challenge that highlights the importance of the communicator: Imagine a middle-aged American, whose name is I.M. Wright, watching television. As the images of a burning American flag flash on television, Mr. Wright hears the insurgents saying that the government has become oppressive, and "it is the right of the people to alter or to abolish it . . . It is their right, it is their duty, to throw off such government!" David Myers suggests that this scene may upset Mr. Wright and lead him to believe that communists have gotten too much air time. However, if our imaginary Mr. Wright were at a July 4th Independence Day rally and the Declaration of Independence was read, including this quote, his reaction would have been quite different. In all likelihood, instead of getting upset over communist aggression, he would beam with patriotic pride.[121]

Thus, a statement that ordinarily would reach us through the central route of persuasion, can take on a fundamentally different meaning depending on who communicates it, creating a peripheral cue that affects the message.

Credibility and Attractiveness

Social psychological research has shown that credibility and attractiveness enhance how effective a person is at communicating: "credible communicators seem both *expert* (confidently knowledgeable) and *trustworthy*."[122] For example, former Surgeon General Dr. C. Everett Koop was chosen to make anti-smoking commercials because he was the embodiment of a credible communicator. He was a respected physician who delivered his message with the calm and assured conviction of an expert. Dr. Koop was also a trusted source of information not only because of his office, but also because his demeanor fit the cultural stereotype of one who is trustworthy—a kind grandfather and seasoned doctor with the wisdom brought on by age.

Attractiveness is another major source of influence in enhancing the power of the communicator. While physical appeal is important, please don't think of attractiveness strictly in terms of youthful beauty and sexiness. Similarity is an important factor in trying to influence others.[123] People are attracted to those who are most like them. This attraction extends not just to physical similarity, but also to shared values and judgments. For instance, an elderly, fit and vibrant person touting the benefits of joining the American Association of Retired Persons is going to be more convincing to the target audience than a stunning 20-year-old in tight jeans delivering the same message.

What community association professionals and members can learn from this is that as communicators their message depends on them. Hence, all the professionals dealing with community associations must position themselves as experts. Remember, to be perceived as an expert, one has to be able to communicate knowledge with confidence and conviction. People are more receptive to this sort of expertly delivered message than to one that is not grounded in self-assurance.

Unfortunately, I have observed too many meetings where a community association board goes off on a tangent while the association manager—visibly uncomfortable—sits silent and unwilling to assert their knowledge. These managers ultimately fail to establish themselves as experts. I believe this sort of hesitation might stem from fear of alienating the board and losing the account. However, our society is expert-oriented, and most boards want (and are willing to pay for) an expert manager, not just administrative support.

The Message

Now that we have established the importance of the communicator, the next important aspect is the message itself—its content does matter. I'm sure each of you has, at some point, struggled with how to structure and position your message. In doing so, you have likely asked yourself any of several questions:[124]

First, how much can you deviate from the views that your audience holds? Will you be able to sway more people by adopting an extreme viewpoint or by advocating a perspective that's close to what they already think? The answer to this question depends on the credibility of the communicator. "Highly credible people elicit the greatest opinion changes when they argue an extreme position; less credible people are more successful when they advocate positions close to that of the audience."[125] For example, if an association must levy an unwelcome special assessment, the board may ask the association's CPA or auditor to present the case to the homeowners at the annual meeting. Hence, community association managers and other professionals serving the industry who establish themselves as experts with high credibility can accomplish much in bringing positive change to the communities that they manage.

Second, should your message represent only the perspectives of your side, or should it address the views of the other, often adversarial, side? On this issue, David Myers argues that, "when the audience already agrees with the message, is unaware of opposing arguments, and is unlikely later to consider the opposition, then a one-sided appeal is most effective. With more sophisticated audiences or with those not already agreeing, two-sided messages are most successful."[126]

In terms of this issue in advertising products, think of the Pepsi commercials that use Coca-Cola products for comparison. Are they truly convincing? Do they make their point or do they possibly spend their advertising dollars on providing free advertising for their rival products? Do Coca-Cola devotees become Pepsi converts as a result of these commercials? Or is it possible that those who have made up their minds on these products will remain entrenched in their original positions?

While the jury may be out on the Pepsi-Coke rivalry, when it comes to articulating the opposing views or ignoring them in the context of community associations, the situation may be somewhat different. For example, I remember sitting in on a board meeting that ran for four hours because four community association management companies were being interviewed for a new contract. At the end of this exhausting process the board members' consensus was that one of the companies was a clear winner. Although this was the only company that was a member of CAI and touted it as an added value, that wasn't the main reason this company came across so favorably in everyone's opinion. The difference was that this was the only company that acknowledged alternative forms of management and explained why it did not necessarily espouse them. The representatives of this company were also very cognizant of what their competition did, and they were not afraid to address their differences with their rivals. It was very impressive that they were able to do this in terms that sounded objective and not disparaging. Hence, acknowledging opposing or differing perspectives should be done with assurance, and the information should be delivered with grace and dignity.

Third, who has the advantage in community meetings or other forums where opposing views are presented—those who go first or those who go last? Research shows that "information presented early is often the most potent, especially when it affects one's interpretation of later information. However, if a time gap separates the two sides, the effect of the early information diminishes; if a decision is also made right after hearing the second side, which is still fresh in mind, the advantage will likely go to the second presentation."[127]

Consequently, the order in which the audience is presented with the message is important. In light of community association management issues, remembering this is very important. For instance, I recall sitting in on meetings when a community association board had to select a general contractor for a major construction project. They interviewed one prospective contractor each week for three consecutive weeks. The portfolios of these general contractors were quite similar. Yet the board decided to go with the one they interviewed in the third and final week, i.e., the one they saw last. Although many factors were considered in making this decision, it's hard to think that the order and the time between the interviews didn't affect the board's choice of the contractor that appeared last.

How the Message is Delivered

When it comes to delivering the message, the environment and the feelings that it arouses also play an important role. Many people live in a world of individual mental associations where an item or an aroma will kindle positive memories and feelings. That's why realtors tell their clients who are trying to sell their homes to bake bread, light vanilla-scented candles, and leave out cookies. These images epitomize the warmth associated with a loving family. Similarly, CEOs of major corporations close multi-million dollar deals with a handshake as they finish a game of golf. And just about everyone has had lunch with someone at which important business propositions or career changes were discussed.

The Power of Feeling Good

All of these examples deal with positive settings in which we feel good and enjoy ourselves. Thus, it's important to remember the power of good feelings when attempting to sway the opinion of an audience. For instance, in one experiment Yale University "students were more convinced by persuasive messages if they were allowed to enjoy peanuts and Pepsi while reading them."[128] The simple explanation for this is that "good feelings enhance persuasion, partly by enhancing positive thinking (when people are motivated to think) and partly by linking good feelings with the message."[129]

When people are in a good mood, they're more optimistic and have a kinder disposition. Each of us can recall times when we have been more forgiving and tolerant when we were in a good mood. Also, when in a good mood, people "make faster, more impulsive decisions; they rely more on peripheral cues. Unhappy people ruminate more before reacting, so they are less easily swayed by weak arguments."[130]

It's important to ensure that the audience is in a good mood. Indeed, many public speakers begin their presentations with personal anecdotes, jokes, or inspiring stories because they know that a relaxed and cheerful audience will be more open and receptive to their message. The practical lesson for community associations is that perhaps it's a good idea to take steps to make homeowners feel positive and comfortable at association meetings that are likely to be steeped in controversy—offer refreshments, ensure that the lighting is adequate, the temperature is comfortable, and that the seats are comfortable. The good feelings that a pleasant environment and refreshments might arouse may take the edge off of a sharp confrontation.

Space and spatial arrangements are also important considerations for arousing good feelings. One association learned that simply changing the configuration of the room improved the mood at the annual meeting. By eliminating the head table and having the board members sit among the homeowners, they shifted the mood from "them and us" to "they *are* us."

The Power of Fear

A popular expression says that you can bait flies better with honey than vinegar. But what if honey—a pleasant environment—doesn't work? Can fear be used as an effective form of persuasion? The answer is "Yes."

Much advertising regarding public and personal health issues is based on fear. In an experiment testing the power of fear doctors sent "a letter to their patients who smoked. Of those who received a positively framed message (explaining that by quitting they would live longer) 8 percent tried to quit smoking. Of those who received a fear-framed message (explaining that by continuing to smoke they would likely die sooner), 30 percent tried to quit."[131] While I personally have a hard time condoning anything based on fear, I have to acknowledge that people do react to it.

However, fear-driven messages aren't guaranteed to succeed. "People might respond with denial, because if they aren't told how to avoid the danger, the frightening messages can be overwhelming. Fear-arousing messages are more effective if you lead people not only to fear the severity and likelihood of a threatened event but also to perceive an effective protective strategy."[132] Obviously, this concept has been used effectively by the security industry and by real estate developers to convince millions of Americans that gated communities are the answer to their threatened sense of security. Indeed, it's estimated that the number of gated communities (with fences and guard stations restricting access) has increased nearly tenfold in the last 30 years.

The Audience

It's impossible to talk about the powers of persuasion without taking into account the audience.

Age

The sociopolitical attitudes that people hold tend to vary depending on their age.[133] There are two basic explanations for such differences—a life-cycle explanation and a generational explanation.[134] The life-cycle explanation claims that people's attitudes change as they grow older, while the generational explanation argues that people tend to hold the views and attitudes that they adopted in their young and formative years. As a new generation grows and shapes its attitudes, the views between different generations differ and result in a generation gap.

Thus, it's important to consider the audience's prevailing value system. For instance, a real estate developer marketing a 55+ community would use tactics different from those targeting an audience of first-time homebuyers with young children. Likewise, a community association manager might use different messages depending on the board composition of various clients.

Receptivity

In speaking of the powers of persuasion, we should also consider how receptive the audience is to the message. If an audience has advance knowledge or is expecting a message, they have time to build counter arguments, and this may make them more resistant. David Myers refers to this as "forewarned is forearmed."[135] He cites an experiment, where a group of California high school students were to hear a "talk entitled 'Why Teenagers Should Not Be Allowed to Drive.' Those forewarned did not budge. Others, not forewarned, did."[136] Clearly, this has implications for community associations as well. For instance, a board member might get better results by presenting a radical proposal right at a meeting rather than broaching the idea with the board members prior to the meeting. If other board members, who may resist the ideas, are exposed to them in advance, they'll have time to build strong counter arguments that they can use at the meeting when the idea is presented publicly. I'm speaking, of course, in general terms. Board members should use discretion and not shock other group members without fair warning.

Corporations and even the federal government avoid shocking the public by leaking information to test the reaction of their employees, the legislators, and the public to radical new proposals. This strategy tests whether the audience is receptive to the message and identifies its counter arguments.

Counter-arguing diminishes when "verbal persuasion is enhanced by distracting people with something that attracts their attention just enough to inhibit counter-arguing."[137] For instance, when a presentation is made using high technology, the audience may be less able to counter the message if the visual effects are spectacular.

I observed this when an association board attended a presentation by an interior decorator and ended up committing to a project that was way above their budget. The interior decorator had done such a good job presenting different samples, color palettes, and renditions that it was hard for the board to resist the proposed project.

CHAPTER 7

Mental Shortcuts Used in Groups

Alfred North Whitehead noted that, "Civilization advances by extending the number of operations we can perform without thinking about them."[138] Thinking, or our sometimes unconscious desire not to, is indeed key when it comes to understanding how the weapons of influence work.

How the Brain Works

To gain insight into our thinking, it is important to know how our brain functions. In 1990, Presidential Proclamation 6158 declared the 1990s to be the decade of the brain. It noted,

> The human brain, a 3-pound mass of interwoven nerve cells that controls our activity, is one of the most magnificent—and mysterious—wonders of creation. The seat of human intelligence, interpreter of senses, and controller of movement, this incredible organ continues to intrigue scientists and laymen alike.
>
> Over the years, our understanding of the brain—how it works, what goes wrong when it is injured or diseased—has increased dramatically. However, we still have much more to learn.[139]

Indeed, the complexity of the brain is mind-boggling—it "is still the most amazing functional system in the world. We carry around in that small package a machine capable of storing and analyzing more information than the most powerful supercomputers. It might not be as fast at repetitive calculations, but it is able to deal simultaneously with thousands of kinds of input, select the important from the unimportant, and process images in ways unmatched by the most complex video devices."[140] I remember reading in a scholarly publication that the neural connections of our brains are longer than all of the world's phone networks combined.

Despite its immense complexity, the brain strives for simplicity. One way it does this is with mental shortcuts. Stereotypes, for example, are mental shortcuts. For instance, when we cast an association board member or a resident as a troublemaker, then this stereotype enables us to make quick decisions about the

How the Mind Creates Shortcuts

Try these four experiments with groups of ten or more people. Be sure to instruct them to respond to your instructions quickly.

Experiment 1: Ask one person to be a respondent in this game of bizarre spelling. You will spell a word, and the respondent will have to immediately pronounce it. Do a warm-up exercise. For instance, spell "d-o-g" and have them quickly respond "dog," spell "c-a-t" and have them once again quickly respond "cat." Now start spelling the following words, "M-a-c-D-o-n-a-l-d," "M-a-c-I-n-t-o-s-h," "M-a-c-G-o-v-e-r-n," "M-a-c-D-o-u-g-a-l," and, finally, "M-A-C-H-I-N-E-R-Y." Nine times out of ten, the respondent will pronounce the last word as "MacHinery," in the form of a Scottish last name, rather than "machinery," meaning a piece of equipment.

Experiment 2: Inform the group that you're going to say a number, and they are to respond with the number immediately following. Once again, they should be very prompt in their responses. Start with small numbers, such as "4," they respond "5." You say "16," they say "17," etc. Avoid using any number that ends in 9. Increase the numbers 121, 143, 384, 576, 1234, 2371, 3863, until you end with 4099. Once again, nine times out of ten the group will say "5000" in response to "4099."

Experiment 3: In this experiment the group pronounces out loud what you spell. Once again, instruct the group to respond quickly. Start by using a simple example such as "c-a-t," then proceed to spell words like "s-o-a-k," "p-o-l-k," "y-o-k-e," "c-o-k-e," "j-o-k-e," and quickly ask, "What do you call the white of the egg?" The majority of the people will answer "yolk."

Experiment 4: Ask the respondents to be very prompt in answering your questions. Start out by showing them something colorful, and ask them to identify the color. Then proceed to objects that are all white, such a sheet of paper, possibly a wall, a piece of clothing, and ask the group to identify the color. Then quickly ask them "What do cows drink?" Most people will answer "milk," because their brains will associate milk with the color white.

suggestions, thoughts, and actions of that person without much further deliberation. Most readers are thinking, no, we surely aren't like that; but, to observe the brain taking mental shortcuts, try the experiments listed below.

As the experiments show, our minds are very efficient and create shortcuts for interpreting certain information, almost by compartmentalizing that information into categories. The members of your group are undoubtedly competent enough to read words like "machinery," count properly, know that 4100 follows 4099, distinguish between egg whites and yolks, and, finally, know that cows drink water not milk. However, most of them will likely fall prey to the shortcuts that their brains create. The six principles of influence, which Cialdini calls weapons of influence, are based on the brain's tendency to create mental shortcuts.

Fixed-Action Patterns

Our behavior and our mental responses are often based in fixed-action patterns. "A fundamental characteristic of these patterns is that the behaviors comprising them occur in virtually the same fashion and in the same order every time."[141] Animals and people both exhibit fixed-action patterns.

Fixed-action patterns were demonstrated in an experiment with a turkey hen and a stuffed polecat—a turkey hen's natural enemy. Under normal circumstances even a stuffed and motionless polecat provokes a violent reaction from a hen. However, when "the same stuffed replica [of a polecat] carried inside it a small recorder that played the cheep-cheep sound of baby turkeys, the mother not only accepted the oncoming polecat but gathered it underneath her. When the machine was turned off, the polecat model again drew a vicious attack."[142]

Robert Cialdini calls the turkey's response a "click-whirr reaction." He argues that "It is almost as if the patterns were recorded on tapes within the animals. When a situation calls for courtship, a courtship tape gets played; when a situation calls for mothering, a maternal behavior tape gets played. *Click* and the appropriate tape is activated; *whirr* and out rolls the standard sequence of behaviors."[143] Surely I'm not comparing people to turkeys, but people exhibit fixed-action patterns just the same.

Mental Shortcut: Because

"A well-known principle of human behavior says that when we ask someone to do us a favor we will be more successful if we provide a reason. People simply like to have reasons for what they do."[144] Social psychologist Ellen Langer and her colleagues demonstrated this principle by testing people's behavior in a line at a copy machine. When a person approached the line at a library copy machine and said, "Excuse me, I have five pages. May I use the Xerox machine because I'm in a rush?" The request was granted 94 percent of the time.[145] When the same question was asked and "because I'm in a rush" was dropped, the success diminished to 60 percent. So far, no stunning surprises. However, when the question was rephrased yet again and simply ended with the word "because" with no further explanation, the success rate climbed to 93 percent. Apparently, "just as the cheep-cheep sound of turkey chicks triggered an automatic mothering response from mother turkeys, even when it emanated from a stuffed polecat, so the word because triggered an automatic compliance response from Langer's subjects, even when they were given no subsequent reason to comply. *Click, whirr.*"[146]

Mental Shortcut: Expensive Equals Good

Robert Cialdini likens the response of the people in line for the copy machine to the behavior of the customers at his friend's Indian jewelry store in Arizona. This woman had some turquoise jewelry inventory that just wouldn't move, so before she went out of town she left written instructions for her assistant to mark the jewelry at half price to get rid of the inventory. To her delight, the assistant misinterpreted her handwriting and marked the jewelry up at twice its price. The miraculous result—it was sold out by the time the store owner returned. Cialdini explains the sell-out of the jewelry by the fact that "the customers, mostly well-to-do vacationers, with little knowledge of turquoise, were using a standard principle—a stereotype—to guide their buying: expensive = good. Much research shows that people who are unsure of an item's quality often use this stereotype."[147] Community association attorney Marv Nodiff told me recently that his "dad had a retail store for years—tools, machinery, and equipment. He had a rule: if an item didn't sell, paint it a different color, move it to a different spot, or raise the price."

Cialdini argues that the customers basing their judgment on price alone "were playing a shortcut version of betting the odds. Instead of stacking all the odds in their favor by trying painstakingly to master each feature that indicates the worth of turquoise jewelry, they were counting on just one—the one they knew to be usually associated with the quality of any item."[148] Just think how many times boards in community associations engage in betting the odds themselves. I observed a board deciding on a contractor for a major construction project. They did indeed bet the odds on this stereotype. My personal opinion was that one of the other two contractors seemed to offer better services and seemed very motivated to get the account, but the board chose the contractor who had submitted the highest bid. The board reasoned that this contractor wouldn't have been confident enough to submit a high bid if they weren't going to do a good job.

Most people have been victimized by the expensive-equals-good stereotype—good products, good service, good outcomes. Indeed, the marketing philosophy of many companies, such as Tiffany, Armani, and Gucci, capitalizes on this stereotype. Does this stereotype have any relevance, though, for community associations? Yes, it does. While many community association management companies and law firms specializing in community associations struggle to provide the best service at the most competitive rates, there are many other companies that profit from this principle. These companies position themselves as the purveyors of excellence in the industry, and clients follow.

Recently, I was talking with an owner of a community association management company in the Boston area, and this is exactly how he has restructured his company. He told me he had gotten rid of the unprofitable accounts and positioned his company as one that would provide superior service at commensurate rates. Of course, one must be able to attain excellence, not just speak of it. To this association manager's satisfaction this strategy had served him well. Also, many new developments base the marketing of their communities and services on the stereotype that expensive equals good.

Mental Shortcut: Relying on Experts

Psychologists use a sophisticated term to refer to mental shortcuts—judgmental heuristics.[149] "Heuristics" is a fancy philosophical word that means "guiding learning patterns." Our attitude toward experts is a powerful example of the judgment heuristic that "goes [like this], 'If an expert said so, it must be true.' There is an unsettling tendency in our society to accept unthinkingly the statements and directions of individuals who appear to be authorities on the topic. That is, rather than thinking about an expert's arguments and being convinced (or not), we frequently ignore the arguments and allow ourselves to be convinced just by the expert's status as 'expert.' "[150] Once again, this shows the pattern of *click, whirr* creating a mental shortcut.

The social trend to rely on experts has tremendous implications for community associations and the industries supporting them. To an extent, the explosive growth of community associations in the United States can be explained by the trend towards professionalizing our personal lives. An astounding number of people say they chose a community association because someone else would mow the lawn, make sure the place was properly landscaped, and the driveways were paved.

I think children's statements are an interesting representation of social trends. I was talking to a 12-year-old girl about another child who had some adjustment problems at their school. I asked her what, in her opinion, should be done. "Well, they should probably talk to some kind of an expert or a counselor," was her response.

There is an odd contradiction, though, when it comes to professionalization of society and community associations. While a lot of individuals are attracted to community associations for the benefits of having professionals take care of many aspects of their lives, many community association managers fail to position themselves as professionals and share their expertise with association boards. If more community association managers established themselves as the experts and were willing to dispense advice accordingly, the functioning of many groups and boards within the association might improve. Of course, this premise holds true only if the community association managers are true experts who have attained the requisite education and associated designations—such as CMCA®, AMS®, or PCAM®—rather than being self-proclaimed experts. At the same time I should acknowledge that many community association boards are so obsessed with costs that they'll select their experts—whether it's the attorney, the community association manager, the accountant, the engineer, or the landscaper—based on the lowest rate regardless of the quality or level of expertise.

By resorting to mental shortcuts in our daily decision making and functioning, or to the *click, whirr* reactions we use to respond to our environment, we have the advantage of creating "efficiency and economy by reacting automatically to a usually informative trigger feature, [and we] preserve crucial time, energy, and mental capacity."[151] However, the downside is that we become vulnerable to potentially "silly and costly mistakes,"[152] which can often be avoided if greater attention is paid to the process of decision making instead of relying on our automatic reactions. However, just being aware of mental shortcuts and our excessive reliance on them will enable us to be better decision makers.

CHAPTER 8

Weapons of Influence in Groups

The ultimate goal of persuasion is compliance, or, in simpler terms, getting someone to do what you want them to do or to believe what you want them to believe. In order to get others to comply, you must be adept at influencing them. Thus, in a sense, persuasion and influence are the same phenomenon; or, in the very least, they strive for the same outcome.

Social psychologist Robert Cialdini has conducted much research trying to understand how compliance works and why is it that some individuals are more successful than others in persuading people to do what they want. For his research, Ciadini studied people he calls compliance professionals—those who work in the service industry, such as sales clerks in retail stores, car salesmen, waiters and waitresses, and people who work in development.

As a result of his research Robert Cialdini identified six principles on which compliance professionals rely most often to achieve their desired ends. These principles are reciprocity, consistency, social proof, liking, authority, and scarcity. In fact, the impact of these six principles is so formidable that Cialdini calls them "weapons of influence." Understanding these weapons of influence is very important in the context of both individual and group decision making.

Reciprocity

A number of years ago a university professor conducted an experiment by sending Christmas cards to a host of strangers. To his surprise, he got numerous responses from people who didn't even inquire who he was. This is a classic example of a *click, whirr* response.[153] The professor's experiment provides a vivid demonstration of the rule of reciprocity. "The rule says that we should try to repay, in kind, what another person has provided us."[154] Marv Nodiff reminded me of La Rochefoucauld's maxim that we flatter in order to be flattered.

This rule is pervasive. Indeed, it accomplishes a lot of good in our society. However, it also makes us vulnerable to exploitation by other individuals or companies. The rule is a big part of politics and it fuels political contributions. It also plays a role in commerce. For instance, a free sample not only introduces us to the taste or quality of a new product, but it may also make us feel obligated to buy it. *Click, whirr,* reciprocity at work.[155] Despite its overall positive social effects, in a way, the rule can work against us by enforcing uninvited debts and triggering unfair exchanges.[156]

Reciprocal Concessions

The rule of reciprocity can be advantageous when negotiating, because one of its consequences is that it creates an "obligation to make a concession to someone who has made a concession to us."[157] For instance, if you ask someone for a big favor and they turn you down, they are far more likely to grant you a lesser favor. However, they probably wouldn't have agreed to the lesser favor if you had asked for it first. Yet, because you conceded the size of the favor, they conceded to grant it. In essence, people or groups of people engage in reciprocal concessions.

Robert Cialdini calls this a "rejection-then-retreat technique." He tells of a Boy Scout who approached him offering tickets for $5. When Cialdini declined to buy the tickets, the Boy Scout offered chocolate bars for $1. Cialdini bought two. Compared to the $5 tickets, the chocolate bars were a bargain—even though he didn't need them in the first place. He had experienced the "rejection-then-retreat" technique.[158]

Community associations deal with this weapon of influence every day. For example, if the decorating committee recommends that new shutters or awnings should be added to each of the 224 residences in the association, the board may turn them down. On the other hand, if the committee *first* recommends expansive renovations including structural modifications, new thermal-pane windows, *and* new shutters or awnings, the board will surely turn them down. However, the committee now has a very good chance of getting just the shutters or awnings approved in the next round of negotiations with the board.

Also, if a group of owners within the association wants to make changes in the association rules, they're better off asking for something very drastic at the outset. This will make a moderate approach seem acceptable later on.

Much social progress and change has happened because of this rule. Every time radical people or fringe groups push an extreme social agenda they actually define the middle ground. As the middle ground becomes the norm, the unacceptable eventually is accepted.

Commitment and Consistency

After people make a commitment to a cause, project, idea, or decision they are more likely to agree to requests that support it. To understand why this happens, let's look at the theory of cognitive dissonance.

Cognitive Dissonance

While many of us have heard the term "cognitive dissonance," most of us are not fully aware of its meaning. "Cognitive dissonance" describes that unsettling feeling we get when our behavior and our beliefs don't quite go together. The theory of cognitive dissonance was developed by Leon Festinger, who believed that "people experience tension when they hold two inconsistent ideas, and this state creates a drive to reduce the dissonance, or tension."[159] Subconsciously, we like to have consistency between our behaviors and beliefs.

But what comes first—behaviors or beliefs? Most people will say that belief drives behavior. However, the contrary is closer to the truth. Sometimes, by acting in a specific way, we unconsciously adjust our beliefs to avoid cognitive dissonance, a very disconcerting state of mind. Many experiments have demonstrated this point.

For instance, researchers found that only "46 percent of Toronto suburbanites [were] willing to give to cancer [research] when approached directly. Others, asked a day ahead to wear a lapel pin publicizing the drive (which all agreed to do), were nearly twice as likely to donate."[160] This means that after wearing the pin, 92 percent of the people were willing to give money for cancer research.

Consider another similar experiment that was conducted in California, where "researchers posing as safety-drive volunteers asked Californians to permit the installation of a huge, poorly lettered 'Drive Carefully' sign in their front yards. Only 17 percent consented. Others were first approached with a small request: Would they display a 3-inch 'Be a Safe Driver' window sign? Nearly all readily agreed. When approached two weeks later to allow the large, ugly sign in their front yards, 76 percent consented."[161]

This phenomenon is also known as the foot-in-the-door principle, which means that if you can get people to do you a small favor, a big favor might follow.[162] In both experiments, once people had worn the lapel pins and displayed the window decals, they internalized the message of fighting cancer or driving safely. Then, their rejection of the requests to give money for cancer research or to put up an ugly sign in their front yards would have created cognitive dissonance in themselves. Their actions adjusted their beliefs on the issue, and other actions consistent with their newly acquired beliefs followed.

This principle is at work in our community associations as well. For example, for years residents of a condominium association had been asking one particularly well-qualified owner to run for a board position—without success. Then she was asked if she might have time to distribute flyers door to door for an upcoming event. She was willing to help with such a small matter. Next she was asked to sit in on committee meetings occasionally just so they could get her opinion. That was OK. Soon she was attending regularly, and eventually became a member of one of the committees. A year later, she was the chair.

Today she's not only on the board, but she has become the president of the association. She couldn't make the leap onto the board at the outset, but as she internalized the business of the association, she was able to become its leader.

When I try to explain the concept of cognitive dissonance in the classroom, I usually evoke the image of the Bubble Boy who appeared in the sitcom *Seinfeld*. For those of you who may not have followed this sitcom, the Bubble Boy was a central character in one of the episodes. He lived in a special bubble because he was severely allergic to the environment. In a way, we all live in a bubble, constantly trying to adjust our worldviews so that they fit the environment of our bubble. One other way to look at this is to imagine the structure of a mechanical watch. Just as the cogs on the wheels turn each other, so do our behaviors and beliefs move us forward in a state of mutual dependency.

The Importance of Initial Commitments

When it comes to using commitment and consistency as a weapon of influence, "securing an initial commitment is the key. After making a commitment (that is, taking a stand or position), people are more willing to agree to requests that are in keeping with the prior commitment."[163] However, not all initial commitments

---

First One Foot In the Door . . .

The foot-in-the-door phenomenon is more frequent in community association decision making than we would like to admit. Many decisions are made incrementally and result in outcomes that would have been turned down outright had we been presented with them in the beginning.

For instance, owners of a single-family house in a 55+ community association in Maryland asked for a patio. This request sailed through the board's decision making process without any waves. Then, the same owners—who happened to be brother and sister—sought permission to install a jacuzzi on the patio. They argued that the jacuzzi was necessary to alleviate the horrific arthritis pain suffered by their mother who lived with them. This permission too was granted without any hurdles.

What came next gave everyone pause—the patio needed to be enclosed. Apparently mom had social anxiety disorder and was extremely uncomfortable appearing in her swimsuit in an open space. They argued that this was a disability and needed accommodation under the Americans with Disabilities Act.

And so they succeeded in adding an extension to their house—something that never would have been allowed otherwise. The extension now blocked the lake view of two other homes, and the association was attempting to buy the house so it could tear down the extension and resell it. —jm

---

become weapons of influence. "Commitments are most effective when they are active, public, effortful, and viewed as internally motivated (uncoerced)."[164]

"Commitment decisions, even erroneous ones, have a tendency to be self-perpetuating because they 'can grow their own legs.' That is, people often add new reasons and justifications to support the wisdom of commitments that have already been made."[165] Unfortunately, bad policies can result from these self-perpetuating initial commitments. In a way, this situation is similar to the "too much invested to quit phenomenon" described in the section on group polarization.

Robert Cialdini advises that we look to our stomachs and to our hearts "to recognize and resist the undue influence of consistency pressures [i.e., our desire to align our behaviors and beliefs] on our compliance decisions. . . . Stomach signs appear when we realize that we are being pushed by commitment and consistency pressures to agree to requests we know we don't want to perform. . . . Heart-of-heart signs are different. They are best employed when it is not clear to us that an initial commitment was wrongheaded. Here, we should ask ourselves a crucial question, 'Knowing what I know, if I could go back in time, would I make the same commitment?' "[166]

The principle of commitment and consistency is a very powerful weapon of influence. We've all made decisions based on this principle, both in our professional and personal lives. For community associations, it could be innocently hiring a disreputable contractor, or contracting with an association management company that isn't a good fit. For example, a community association board member told me about hiring a contractor to fix the heating system. As various aspects of the project kept going wrong, the association kept paying more money to the contractor to fix things. Then they brought in a neutral company to assess the situation and learned that all the "fixes" had further contributed to the original problem. However, after choosing this contractor, the association had been clearly too committed to their choice to quit.

Just being aware of this weapon of influence is a weapon in itself for associations and professionals to protect themselves.

Social Proof

An "important means that people use to decide what to believe or how to act in a situation is to look at what other people are believing or doing there."[167] That's the principle of social proof, and it's another potent weapon of influence.

We're more susceptible to the principle of social proof than we think, and we employ it more often than we think. How many times have you ordered a particular meal because your friends or family ordered it? How many times have you gone to see a movie because it got wide media coverage? How many times have you purchased a book because your associates at work were reading it?

"We view a behavior as correct in a given situation to the degree that we see others performing it. Whether the question is what to do with an empty popcorn box in a movie theater, how fast to drive on a certain stretch of highway, or how to eat the chicken at a dinner party, the actions of those around us will be important guides in defining the answer."[168]

Our society even has institutions based entirely on the principle of social proof. Sources of information such as *Consumer Reports* (which I relied on yesterday to purchase a television), *The New York Times* bestseller list, Nielsen ratings, and the Better Business Bureau are all official guides catering to our need to find out what others think about specific products and companies.

Uncertainty and Similarity

There are two conditions that make the principle of social proof very powerful—uncertainty and similarity. Whenever there is uncertainty or ambiguity, people will look to those around them for behavioral cues. It's a proven fact that "in ambiguous situations, for instance, the decisions of bystanders to help [in an emergency] are much more influenced by the actions of other bystanders than when the situation is a clear-cut emergency."[169] It's common knowledge among social psychologists that a person's chances of being helped drastically diminish if there are many bystanders. An individual has much better chances of being helped if there are fewer people around. However, in a situation with many people, one person taking action can galvanize many others to step in.

"People are more inclined to follow the lead of similar others." In fact, the inclination to follow people similar to ourselves is so strong that some people have actually committed suicide after being exposed to highly publicized suicide stories of individuals who were similar to themselves. This was proven through statistical research conducted by sociologist David Phillips.[170]

Persuasion

Word-of-mouth advertising, discussed earlier, is not only a potent way to advertise, but it's also a very good form of persuasion. And it's another illustration of the principle of social proof. When we hear about a product from a friend, or we're referred to a service provider by a neighbor, we're taking cues from them. Advertisers produce elaborate infomercials to create the social proof effect by assembling groups of alleged friends or celebrities to persuade you how much they have benefited from a specific product or service. The message is that if it worked for them, it will work for you; if they're satisfied and happy, you'll be satisfied and happy.

Like everyone, community association board members rely on social proof. For example, an association board member recently described to me how the board went about retaining a new association management company: they solicited proposals from seven companies and narrowed their choices down to three whom they interviewed. (So far, their approach sounds fine.) Then they checked references, which is also fine. However, their final decision was based on the anecdotal evidence they had heard from friends who sometimes had only second-hand knowledge about these association management companies. The principle of social proof proved to be stronger than their own impressions.

Robert Cialdini recommends that to be less susceptible to social proof, we should be sensitive to "clearly counterfeit evidence of what similar others are doing and [recognize] that the actions of similar others should not form the sole basis for our decisions."[171] One community association put this advice into practice by implementing a policy that they would check references for prospective employees only *after* the hiring decision was made. The purpose of the reference check was to *confirm* the decision, not influence it.

Cialdini's advice is good for all of us. After all, how many times have you been disappointed by a movie that the media raved about? How many books have let you down even though they were on *The New York Times* bestseller list? And, how many of those meals that your friend was ecstatic about turned out to be a waste of money? Social proof is helpful in guiding us, but we mustn't let it lead us down the wrong path.

Liking

Liking, according to Robert Cialdini, is another powerful weapon of influence. He thinks that much persuasion in many areas of life is based on liking and that, for example, the quintessential Tupperware party strongly capitalizes on this principle of influence as well.[172]

This weapon of influence is based on the premise that "people prefer to say yes to individuals they know and like."[173] People we like have a big influence on us, and that influence is enhanced by such factors as whether someone is attractive, how similar we feel to them, how often they praise us or make us feel good, and how familiar we are with them.

Physical Attractiveness

Generally, we all try to downplay the social importance of good looks. We tell our children that looks aren't everything and books shouldn't be judged by their covers—which is true—but, we don't always follow our own advice.

"That looks count in human affairs is beyond dispute. Studies have shown that people considered attractive fare better with parents and teachers, make more friends and more money, and have better sex with more (and more beautiful) partners. Every year, 400,000 Americans, including 48,000 men, flock to cosmetic surgeons."[174]

Also, "attractive people have more prestigious jobs and make more money."[175] For instance, in one study researchers "looked at the attractiveness of a national sample of Canadians whom interviewers had rated on a 1 (homely) to 5 (strikingly attractive) scale. They found that for each additional unit of attractiveness, people earned, on average, an additional $1,988 annually."[176] When a similar study was conducted in the United States using a sample of 737 MBA graduates, the results revealed that "for each additional scale unit of rated attractiveness, men earned an added $2,600 and women earned an added $2,150."[177]

Physical attractiveness does not translate merely into added earnings across nations, it also "seems to engender a halo effect that extends to favorable impressions of other traits such as talent, kindness, and intelligence. As a result, attractive people are more persuasive both in terms of getting what they request and in changing others' attitudes."[178]

Similarity and Praise

Other factors that enhance how much we like another person are similarity and praise. Similarity is as potent a factor for the principle of liking as it is for the principle of social proof. As for praise, recall how pleased you may have been when someone praised your work or your appearance.[179] However, insincere or excessive praise and compliments produce the opposite result.

Familiarity

Contrary to the old axiom that familiarity breeds contempt, familiarity is more likely to breed positive feelings—once you get to know people, you like them. Cialdini argues that this is particularly true "when the contact takes place under positive rather than negative circumstances."[180] Associations, especially positive ones, also work to enhance liking.[181] Remember the discussion above on peripheral cues in advertising and the marketers' desire to promote positive feelings and associations? It's no wonder that community association marketing materials show breathtaking vistas, manicured and landscaped lawns, happy smiling children, and beautiful women. These pictures establish a positive association between the concept of living in a community association and the attractions that might be linked with a life there.

Liking Too Much

Liking someone too much can mislead people and cause them to act in ways that aren't prudent. For instance, one condominium had a superintendent who clearly was not performing up to appropriate standards. But the board, particularly a couple of its influential members, wouldn't do anything about the situation because they really liked the superintendent.

Since the principle of liking is so strong, it can be difficult to escape. Robert Cialdini recommends separating the message from the messenger. "Upon recognizing that we like a requester inordinately well under the circumstances, we should step back from the social interaction, mentally separate the requester from his or her offer, and make any compliance decision solely on the merits of the offer."[182]

Authority

What Stanley Milgram learned from his experiments on obedience to authority became the basis of Robert Cialdini's analysis of authority. (See the discussion of Milgram's experiments in the section on group conformity.) Indeed, as Milgram showed, the power of authority can push even the most law-abiding individuals to commit acts of atrocity. Robert Cialdini adds that this principle "is frequently adaptive to obey the dictates of genuine authorities because such individuals usually possess high levels of knowledge, wisdom, and power. For these reasons, deference to authorities can occur in a mindless fashion as a kind of decision-making shortcut."[183]

Relying on Experts

In modern-day society authority is closely tied to expertise. In fact, the immense growth of community associations can also be partly explained by the public's growing dependence on experts.

In a way, the proliferation of community associations occurred on a parallel track with the growth of the mutual fund industry in the United States. At the beginning of the 21st century, there are more registered mutual funds than individual stock issues in the United States. This explosive growth of mutual funds is attributed to the widely held and largely justifiable belief that it's better to entrust your money to a professional financial expert than to conduct research and track individual stocks yourself.

Professional Experts for Personal Lives

The proliferation of personal stylists and personal shoppers represents the growing reliance on professional expertise to guide our personal lives. A recent article in *The New York Times* told how David Neuman, the president of Touchstone Television, who was at a loss when selecting his clothes, engaged the services of Deborah Waknin, a personal shopper. According to the article, "neither Mr. Neuman nor Ms. Waknin said they considered it ironic that a man who can run a company should be so baffled by casual Fridays."[184]

Membership in the Association of Image Consultants has grown to 600 from only 100 in 1990.[185] Image consultants are paid, on average, $150 an hour to tell others what to wear, how to style their hair, what colors to avoid—they even select eye wear, jewelry, and other accessories. Susan Ashbrook, the former publicity director for the designer Richard Tyler, explains, "There are so many choices out there, and people have so little time."[186]

In this same frame of mind, many people buy into community associations—the experts will take better care of the lawn and the siding than they can, or because they prefer to spend their time on other things.

In the words of Prof. Leonard Buckle, "We are dealing with increased professionalization of people's personal lives." Indeed, people seem to be hiring out more and more of what used to be strictly personal responsibilities; and, in general, this is good news for the community association industry. However, it can be bad news for many individuals living in community associations who are victimized by false claims of sometimes self-proclaimed experts.

Symbols

People can be fooled by self-proclaimed experts because they have a *click, whirr* reaction toward many symbols that are associated with "authority rather than to its substance. Three kinds of symbols that have been shown by research to be effective in this regard are titles, clothing, and automobiles."[187] Titles can take the form of educational degrees, certifications, and similar forms of credentials.

For instance, a community association may end up retaining an association management company because it claims to have the right educational credentials. But those credentials *may* be from the Mail Order University of Condo Management. This opens up an issue of national or at least state credentialing standards that is beyond the scope of this book but that merits much attention.

Knowledge and Trust

An expert must be not only knowledgeable but also trustworthy in order to be perceived as credible. Robert Cialdini warns of a trick to establish trustworthiness that involves a "trust-enhancing tactic in which a communicator first provides some mildly negative information about him- or herself. Through this strategy the person creates a perception of honesty that makes all subsequent information seem more credible to observers."[188]

To illustrate this case, Cialdini cites the story of Vincent the waiter. Vincent's customers always ordered the most; and, consequently, he got larger tips. Cialdini noticed that Vincent's demeanor differed according to the demographics of his customers. He would be effervescent with a family with children and formal with an older married couple—he altered his messages and delivery according to his audience.

However, Vincent worked his greatest trick with large parties of 8 to 12 people. Cialdini writes:

> His technique was veined with genius. When it was time for the
> first person, normally a woman, to order, he went into his act.
> No matter what she elected, Vincent reacted identically: His
> brow furrowed, he (sic) hand hovered over his order pad, and

after looking quickly over his shoulder for the manager, he leaned conspiratorially toward the table to report for all to hear "I'm afraid that is not as good tonight as it normally is. Might I recommend instead the _____ or the _____?" (At this point Vincent suggested a pair of menu items that were slightly less expensive than the dish the patron had selected initially.) "They are both excellent tonight."

With this single maneuver Vincent engaged several important principles of influence. First, even those who did not take his suggestions felt that Vincent had done them a favor by offering valuable information to help them order. Everyone felt grateful, and consequently, the rule for reciprocity would work in his favor when it came time for them to decide on his gratuity. Besides hiking the percentage of his tip, Vincent's maneuver also placed him in a favorable position to increase the size of the party's order. It established him as an authority on the current stores of the house: he clearly knew what was and wasn't good that night. Moreover—and here is where seeming to argue against his own interests comes in—it proved him to be a trustworthy informant because he recommended dishes that were slightly less expensive than the one originally ordered. Rather than trying to line his own pockets, he seemed to have the customers' best interests at heart.

To all appearances, he was at once knowledgeable and honest, a combination that gave him great credibility. Vincent was quick to exploit the advantage of this credible image.[189]

Indeed, Vincent does sound like a genius resorting to so many weapons of influence all at once. Actually, as I write this, I'm trying to imagine what Vincent himself would think of Robert Cialdini analyzing his behavior. Most of all, I'm wondering if his actions were instinctive or if he methodically thought out his plan. In any case, Vincent's story is a striking demonstration of how susceptible we are to the real or perceived power of authority. Truly, authority can be a potent weapon of influence.

How can we shield ourselves from the negative effects of this influence? Robert Cialdini cautions us always to ask ourselves how legitimate is the expertise of the authority we are dealing with.[190] I guess he would want you to remember Vincent's story as well.

As for me, I wish that we'd all remember Milgram's experiments—there are no boundaries to the destructive powers of misappropriated authority. Like others, many boards of community associations have succumbed to this weapon of influence. Sometimes, they make unreasonable rules or they institute unwise practices. These are the stories that become fodder for the media, ultimately, casting all community associations in the wrong light.

Scarcity

"According to the scarcity principle, people assign more value to opportunities when they are less available."[191] Indeed, we're very susceptible to it, and our society embraces this power of influence with a vengeance. Remember the Beanie Baby epidemic (I was a willing victim myself), or the Pokémon craze, or the Tamagochi madness? I could go on and on, but all I'd be doing is listing marketing campaigns that successfully capitalized on the principle of scarcity.

According to Robert Cialdini, there are two things that make the scarcity principle effective.

If It's Scarce, It Must Be Valuable

"First, because things that are difficult to attain are typically more valuable, the availability of an item or experience can serve as a shortcut cue to its quality."[192]

We have all experienced this firsthand: Collectors, whether hobbyists or professionals, rely on the scarcity principle to add value and interest to their activities. Retailers make "limited time offers," have "one-day sales," deliberately limit quantities, or label ordinary merchandize as "collector's items."

The scarcity principle is used effectively by some cooperatives when the board interviews prospective buyers. Comedian Jerry Seinfeld complained to the media that, while the entire nation knew who he was, the board of his cooperative in New York City needed to interview him and find out if he was fit to walk the 20 feet from the lobby entrance to the elevator. In effect, this board was trying to impress on a celebrity what a special, rare—and scarce—opportunity would be bestowed upon him if they allowed him to live there.

One association management company that I know of benefits from the scarcity principle by positioning itself as hard to get into—like prep school. It turns down potential clients on the grounds that they're just not prepared to deal with this company's exacting standards. This "exclusiveness" strategy can work, provided the company actually delivers exceptional service.

The Effect of Loss

The second reason why the principle of scarcity works as an effective weapon of influence, according to Cialdini, is that "as things become less accessible, we lose freedoms. According to psychological reactance theory, we respond to the loss of freedoms by wanting to have them (along with the goods and services connected with them) *more* than before."[193]

Indeed, it's human nature to want what we lose—even if we didn't particularly want it in the first place. In one case, a community association board was debating whether to renew their landscaping contract—they weren't convinced they were getting their money's worth. The landscaper, however, announced it was dropping its residential customers and focusing entirely on commercial properties. Suddenly, the board decided it couldn't possibly get the level of service it wanted from anyone else, and actually offered to pay *more* if this landscaper would keep them as a client.

Limited Information

Research has shown that "the scarcity principle also applies to the way that information is evaluated. Research indicates that the act of limiting access to a message causes individuals to want to receive it more and to become more favorable to it. The latter of these findings—that limited information is more persuasive—seems the more surprising. In the case of censorship, this effect occurs even when the message has not been received. When a message has been received, it is more effective if it is perceived as consisting of exclusive information."[194]

Examples of this concept can be seen on an international scale as well as at the community association level. Some will remember how *Samizdat*—or "self-published" literature—proliferated in the former Soviet Union, and how the ranks of dissidents were increased as a result of government's censorship of the press.

Of course, community associations are certainly not totalitarian regimes; nevertheless, this research has shown that we value information just because it's scarce. The important lesson for community associations is simple: don't make information scarce. Secrecy will inevitably create conflict in the community. That's why it's important to hold open meetings, post minutes, and make financial information available to the residents. Keeping the association constantly informed is a good idea. Newsletters and association web sites can be very helpful to imbue residents with a sense of community and belonging. At the same time, if the information is presented in such a way that people get a feeling of exclusivity, this too will further enhance the strength of community.

Robert Cialdini thinks that it is very hard to build defenses again the principle of scarcity. Perhaps the best thing to do is to remember that scarcity applies pressure, and to take the time to evaluate why you yearn for whatever you yearn for.

Robert Cialdini suggests that "although we all wish to make the most thoughtful, fully considered decision possible in any situation, the changing form and accelerating pace of modern life frequently deprive us of the proper conditions for such a careful analysis of all the relevant pros and cons. More and more, we are forced to resort to another decision-making approach—a shortcut approach to which the decision to comply (or agree, or believe, or buy) is made on the basis of a single, usually reliable piece of information."[195] The more mental shortcuts we make, the more we use—and expose ourselves to—weapons of influence.

Conclusion

So, now that you've read these chapters and you're on your way to a board or staff meeting, remember that to be at your best, and to bring the group up to its best, you must be aware of the dynamics and influences that occur in group settings.

- Be cognizant of the group size.
- Clarify for yourself how you relate to the group; what is the importance of that group in your life? Remember, this affects what you expect from the group.
- Be aware of the group's leader and leadership style. And if you are that leader, ask yourself if there is any room for improvement.
- Assess the possible patterns in your group that lead to either increased or decreased risk-taking in the decision-making process.
- Share your arguments with the group in an objective manner by separating your feelings from the facts.
- On the other hand, remember that if you're very passionate on a given issue, and you need to sway the opinion of the group, only an impassioned plea has a chance of working. Otherwise, keep in mind that mild and polite arguments will result in attitude inoculation on the part of group members.
- Evaluate the nature of your group—is it cohesive or not? If it's cohesive, ask yourself if this cohesiveness comes at the expense of flawed decision-making resulting from groupthink.
- Evaluate the decision-making procedures that the group has in place. For instance, if you'd get three different bids for a paving or a plumbing job, then why not discuss at least three different approaches to solving the problems that might be on the agenda?
- Pay attention to the techniques of persuasion that are being used by you or by other members of the group.
- Evaluate whether you're being unduly coerced to make certain decisions or if you're avoiding making certain decisions.
- Think of the mental shortcuts you may have made by classifying your neighbors and other association members into troublemakers and peace-

makers, bad ones and good ones. Try to reassess the labels that you might
have given to the different people in the community, and try to view their
position and their arguments outside these labels.

■ Above all, remember that groups affect our individual behavior.

The information that I've presented in this book is meant to provide those
in community associations—primarily board members and managers, but also
the many professionals who work with them—with a general roadmap into
very complex territory. Just remember that real-life situations aren't always on
the map.

Postscript

Life would be so bland if we all made the apt decisions on the first pass.
—David Brudnoy[196]

In this book I have attempted to present findings of socio-psychological research which help explain why smart people sometimes make really stupid decisions. Hard as it is to accept, we aren't always guided by our independent thinking. All of us are very susceptible to the power of situations. Within group settings, the effects of that power are amplified.

While this book is intended specifically for residents of community associations and the professionals who serve community associations, everybody would benefit from a knowledge of group influences on our decision-making.

I realize that I've used many examples of bad decisions that were made by community associations. This is not to imply that bad decisions are the norm in community associations. Indeed, that is not the case. There are thousands of associations where people make good decisions, build solid communities, and live in harmony. However, they rarely get media coverage. It's the associations that are stewed in conflict that tend to seize the limelight.

This, however, doesn't apply to community associations exclusively. For instance, there is 200 times more research on depression than on happiness. Before you blame researchers for this imbalance, consider that perhaps this is a reflection of our social values and what we are conditioned to notice. I'm sure that in your daily work, as an attorney, an accountant, a community association manager, or any other professional you are more likely to hear complaints on your missteps than congratulations for a job well done. It's a well-established fact that negative news sells and positive news tanks. Many publications dedicated to promoting positive materials have gone under. Hence, we should be cognizant of our tendency to focus on the negative without paying due attention to what may be positive. Once the negative worldview starts prevailing, organizations—community associations are organizations too—may commit missteps by eliminating positive things in the process of their realignment (this is akin to the metaphor of throwing the baby out with the bath water).

It's time for us to take notice of those trends and to take action. Do something nice, thank somebody for a job well done, and celebrate the good decisions you've made. Celebrate also your community keeping things in perspective. And if you need help with perspective, read the letter below.

Dear Mother and Dad,

Since I left for college…I am sorry for my thoughtlessness in not having written before. I will bring you up to date now, but before you read on, please sit down. You are not to read any further unless you are sitting down, OK?

Well, then, I am getting along pretty well now. The skull fracture and the concussion I got when I jumped out the window of my dormitory when it caught on fire shortly after my arrival here is pretty well healed now. I only spent two weeks in the hospital, and now I can see almost normally and only get those sick headaches once a day. Fortunately, the fire in the dormitory, and my jump, was witnessed by an attendant at a gas station near the dorm, and he was the one who called the Fire Department and the ambulance. He also visited me in the hospital and since I had nowhere to live because of the burnt-out dormitory, he was kind enough to invite me to share his apartment with him. It's really a basement room, but it's kind of cute. He is a very fine boy, and we have fallen deeply in love and are planning to get married. We haven't set the exact date yet, but it will be before my pregnancy begins to show.

Yes, Mother and Dad, I am pregnant. I know how much you are looking forward to being grandparents, and I know you will welcome the baby and give it the same love and devotion and tender care you gave me when I was a child. The reason for the delay in our marriage is that my boyfriend has a minor infection which prevents us from passing our premarital blood tests and I carelessly caught it from him. He is kind, and although not well educated, he is ambitious.

Now that I have brought you up to date, I want to tell you that there was no dormitory fire, I did not have a concussion or skull fracture, I was not in the hospital, I am not pregnant, I am not engaged, I am not infected, and there is no boyfriend. However, I am getting a 'D' in American History and an 'F' in Chemistry, and I want you to see those marks in their proper perspective.

Your loving daughter, Sharon[197]

And as you keep things in perspective, act on what you believe. Ultimately, I would like to share with you what my 15-year-old daughter, Susan, told me, "Footprints in the sand of time are not made by sitting down."

—JM

Glossary

Aggregates: Collections of people who share space, but not social status.

Authoritarian (Leadership Style): Seen in those who take charge and personally control situations; very directive, insist on strict accountability from group members; is essential if projects are to be completed.

Co-housing: A type of collaborative housing that attempts to overcome the alienation of modern subdivisions in which no one knows their neighbors.

Confirmation Bias: A tendency to search for information that confirms one's preconceptions.

Categories: Collections of people who share social status, but not space.

Cognitive Dissonance: Tension experienced when a person holds two inconsistent ideas.

Comparative Function: Enables us to assess ourselves in relation to others.

Democratic (Leadership Style): Seen in those who rely on group participation and input.

Dyad: The smallest group, consists of two people, a pair.

Expert: Someone who combines confidence with knowledge and is willing to communicate his or her message.

Expressive Leadership: Seen in those who inspire and motivate the group in general.

Fixed-Action Patterns: Behaviors that occur in virtually the same fashion and in the same order every time.

Foot-in-the-Door Principle: If you can get people to do you a small favor, a big favor might follow.

Group: Two or more people who identify with one another and regularly interact and feel some sense of solidarity or common identity.

Group Cohesion: The overall strength of positive relationships within the group; the sum of all pressures acting to keep individuals in a group.

Group Composition: The nature and background of its members.

Group Dynamics: A "field of inquiry dedicated to advancing knowledge about the nature of groups, the laws of their development, and their interrelations with individuals, other groups, and larger institutions.

Group Leadership: The process by which certain individuals mobilize and guide groups.

Group Polarization: A tendency for group discussion to enhance the individuals' initial leanings.

Groupthink: Signs of high cohesiveness and an accompanying concurrence-seeking tendency that interfere with critical thinking; strivings for unanimity override the motivation to realistically appraise alternative courses of action; a deterioration of mental efficiency, reality testing, and moral judgment that results from in-group pressures.

Heterogeneous Groups: People with disparate and dissimilar backgrounds.

Homogeneous Grouping: Like-minded people come closer together strengthening their sense of being the in-group, clearly distinct from the other side—the out-group.

Homogeneous Groups: People with very similar backgrounds.

Informational Influence: The group receives information that shifts it away from the dominant viewpoint.

In-Groups, Out-Groups: "An in-group is a social group commanding a member's esteem and loyalty. An out-group, by contrast, is a social group toward which one feels competition or opposition. In-groups and out-groups are based on the idea that 'we' have valued traits that 'they' lack."

Instrumental Leadership: Seen in those who focus on completing specific goals.

Laissez-faire (Leadership Style): Seen in those who are very hands-off and, in general, fail to provide any clear sense of direction to group members.

Mental Shortcuts: Brain functions that save time and mental energy by reacting automatically to an informative trigger.

Normative Function: Anything that provides guidance concerning how to act.

Normative Influence: Decisions, judgments, positions shift from exposure to others' choices.

Out-Groups: See in-groups.

Primary Groups: Those characterized by intimate face-to-face association and cooperation.

Reciprocal Concession: An obligation to make a concession to someone who has made a concession to us.

Reference Group: Those that provide benchmarks for assessing performance and guidelines of how to act.

Satisficing: Deciding on satisfactory levels for some (but not all) attributes of an outcome; identifying one or two criteria that are most important and focusing attention on meeting these criteria.

Scarcity Principle: People assign more value to opportunities when they are less available.

Secondary Groups: Characterized by focus on a common goal; not an end in themselves, rather they are a means to an end.

Social Leadership: Seen in those who inspire and motivate the group in general.

Social Proof: Deciding what to believe or do by looking at what others are doing.

Task Leadership: Seen in those who focus on completing specific goals.

Triad: Three people.

Endnotes

1. This was not necessarily the behavior of the average condominium buyer. Later while interviewing people, I found that many condominium buyers do not go through the trouble of reading the condominium documents, rules, and regulations. Instead, their attorney's tell them that they are standard condominium documents. However, on the other hand, there are people who enroll in special adult education classes on buying a condominium.

2. Macionis, John J., *Society: the Basics*, 5th Ed. (Upper Saddle River, NJ: Prentice Hall, 2000), p. 107.

3. Lindsey, Linda L. and Stephen Beach, *Sociology: Social Life and Social Issues* (Upper Saddle River, NJ: Prentice Hall, 2000), p. 90.

4. Luft, Joseph, *Group Processes: An Introduction to Group Dynamics*, 3rd Ed. (Palo Alto, CA: Mayfield Publishing Company, 1984), p. 7.

5. Lindsey and Beach, op. cit., p. 91.

6. Macionis, John J. and Nijole V. Benokraitis (eds.), *Seeing Ourselves: Classic, Contemporary, and Cross-Cultural Readings in Sociology*, 4th Ed. (Upper Saddle River, NJ: Prentice Hall, 1998), p. 122.

7. Lindsey and Beach, op. cit., p. 92.

8. Macionis and Benokraitis, op. cit., p. 122.

9. Macionis, op. cit., p. 108.

10. Ibid, p. 113.

11. Macionis and Benokraitis, op. cit., p. 123.

12. Coontz, Stephanie, *The Way We Never Were: American Families and the Nostalgia Trap* (New York: Basic Books, a Division of Harper Collins Publishers, 1992), p. 3.

13. Lindsey and Beach, op. cit., p. 93.

14. Luft, op. cit., p. 2.

15. Ibid.

16. Cartwright, Dorwin and Alvin Zander (eds.) *Group Dynamics: Research and Theory*, 2nd Ed. (New York: Harper & Row Publishers, 1960), p. 9.

17. Macionis, op. cit., p. 112.

18. Lindsey and Beach, op. cit., p. 94.

19. Macionis, op. cit., p. 113.

20. Lindsey and Beach, op. cit., p. 95.

21. Baron, Robert S., Norbert L. Kerr and Norman Miller, *Group Process, Group Decision, Group Action* (Pacific Grove, CA: Brooks/Cole Publishing Company, 1992), p. 5.

22. Gladding, Samuel T., *Group Work: A Counseling Specialty*, 3rd Ed. (Upper Saddle River, NJ: Merrill, an Imprint of Prentice Hall, 1999), p. 52.

23. Macionis, op. cit., p. 114.

24. Myers, David G., *Exploring Social Psychology*, 2nd Ed. (Boston: McGraw Hill, 2000), p. 178.

25. Patton, Bobby R. and Kim Giffin, *Problem-Solving Group Interaction* (New York: Harper & Row, Publishers, 1973), p. 68.

26. Ibid.

27. Johnson, David W. and Frank P. Johnson, *Joining Together: Group Theory and Group Skills* (Boston: Allyn & Bacon, 1994), p. 179.

28. Ibid.

29. Ibid.

30. This experiment is described by Solomon Asch in "Effects of Group Pressure upon the Modification and Distortion of Judgments" in Swanson, Guy, Theodore M. Newcomb, & Eugene L. Hartley (eds.), *Readings in Social Psychology* (New York: Holt, Rinehart & Winston, 1952).

31. Lindsey and Beach, op. cit., p. 97.

32. Milgram, Stanley, *Obedience to Authority: An Experimental View* (New York: Harper Torchbooks, 1975), p. 19.

33. Ibid., p. 20.

34. Macionis, op. cit., p. 111.

35. Ibid.

36. Stoner, James, A.F., "Risky and Cautious Shifts in Group Decisions, the Influence of Widely Held Values," Working Paper, Alfred P. Sloan School of Management, Massachusetts Institute of Technology, 1967, Cambridge, MA, p. 1.

37. Stoner, op. cit., p. 2.

38. Myers, op. cit., p. 161.

39. Stoner, op. cit., p. 1.

40. Myers, op. cit., p. 161.

41. Ibid., p. 162.

42. Ibid., p. 163.

43. Phone interview with Elvira Jackson, February 6, 2001.

44. Cited in Myers, David G. and Helmut Lamm, "The Group Polarization Phenomenon" in *Psychological Bulletin*, 1976, Vol. 83, No. 4, 602-627, p. 605.

45. Ibid.

46. Myers, op. cit., p. 164.

47. Kaplan, Martin F., "The Influencing Process in Group Decision Making" in *Group Processes*, Hendrick, Clyde, (ed.) (Newbury Park, CA: Sage Publications, 1987), p. 191.

48. Myers, op. cit., p. 164.

49. Ibid.

50. Ibid., p. 136.

51. Kaplan, loc. cit., p. 190.

52. Myers, op. cit., p. 164-165.

53. Ibid.

54. Kaplan, loc. cit., pp. 190-191.

55. Myers, op. cit., p. 176.

56. Ibid.

57. Ibid., p. 177.

58. Ibid.

59. Patton, Bobby R., Kim Giffin and Eleanor Nyquist Patton, *Decision-Making Group Interaction* (New York: HarperCollins Publishers, 1989), p. 149.

60. Ibid.

61. Ibid, p. 151.

62. Myers, op. cit., p. 152.

63. Janis, Irving L., *Groupthink* (Boston: Houghton Mifflin Company, 1982), p. 7. On a personal note, it was Janis's research that inspired me to call a session I presented at the 1999 CAI conference in Atlanta, Georgia, "Why Groups of Smart People Make Bad Decisions." If session attendance is any indication, then many CAI members were also interested in finding out why really smart people end up making bad decisions as members of small groups.

64. Baron, Kerr, and Miller, op. cit., p. 8.

65. Ibid., p. 9.

66. Janis, op. cit., p. 7.

67. Ibid., p. 9.

68. Ibid.

69. Ibid.

70. Ibid., p. 10.

71. Ibid., p. 245.

72. Ibid., p. 244.

73. Ibid.

74. Ibid., p. 256.

75. Ibid., p. 174.

76. Ibid., p. 220.

77. Ibid.

78. Ibid., p. 174.

79. Ibid., p. 111.

80. Ibid., p. 174.

81. Ibid., p. 113.

82. Ibid., p. 174.

83. Ibid., pp. 36-37.

84. Ibid., p. 59.

85. Ibid., p. 175.

86. Ibid., p. 221.

87. Ibid.

88. Ibid.

89. Ibid.

90. Ibid., p. 175.

91. Ibid., p. 120.

92. Ibid., p. 175.

93. Ibid., p. 118.

94. Ibid.

95. Ibid.

96. Ibid., p. 175.

97. Ibid., p. 40.

98. Ibid., p. 41.

 99.   Ibid., p. 10.

100.   Ibid, p. 262.

101.   Ibid., p. 263.

102.   Myers, op. cit., p. 51.

103.   Janis, op. cit., p. 264.

104.   Ibid., p. 265.

105.   Ibid., p. 266.

106.   Ibid.

107.   Myers, op. cit., p. 121.

108.   Janis, op. cit., p. 267.

109.   Ibid, p. 268.

110.   Ibid, p. 271.

111.   Stokey, Edith and Richard Zeckhauser, *A Primer for Policy Analysis* (New York: W.W. Norton & Company, 1978), p. 124.

112.   Ibid., p. 125.

113.   Ibid.

114.   Ibid.

115.   Kilbourne, Jean and Mary Pipher, *Can't Buy My Love, How Advertising Changes the Way We Think And Feel* (New York: Touchstone Books, 2000).

116.   Krupat, Edward (ed.), *Psychology Is Social, Readings and Conversations in Social Psychology*, 4th Ed. (New York: Longman, 1999), p. 112.

117.   Myers, op. cit., p. 123.

118.   Petty, Richard E., John T. Cacioppo, and David Schumann, "Central and Peripheral Routes to Advertising Effectiveness, the Moderating Role of Involvement" in Krupat, op. cit., p. 125.

119.   Ibid.

120.   Myers, op. cit., p. 120.

121.   Ibid., pp. 120-121.

122.   Ibid., p. 121.

123.   Ibid.

124.   The questions contained in the following three points are a liberal adaptation from Myers, op. cit., p. 123.

125.   Ibid.

126.   Ibid.

127.   Ibid.

128.   Ibid., p. 124.

129.   Ibid.

130.   Ibid.

131.   Ibid., pp. 124-125.

132.   Ibid., p. 125.

133.   Ibid.

134.   Ibid.

135.   Ibid., p. 126.

136. Ibid.

137. Ibid.

138. Cialdini, Robert B., *Influence, Science and Practice*, 3rd Ed. (New York: HarperCollins, 1993), p. 1.

139. Presidential Proclamation 6158, Filed with the Office of the Federal Register, 12, 11 p.m., July 18, 1990, http, //www.loc.gov/loc/brain/.

140. Ray, Oakley and Charles Ksir, *Drugs, Society and Human Behavior*, 8th Ed. (Boston: Mc-Graw-Hill, 1999), pp. 93-94.

141. Cialdini, op. cit., p. 2.

142. Ibid.

143. Ibid., pp. 2-3.

144. Ibid., p. 3.

145. Ibid.

146. Ibid., p. 5.

147. Ibid.

148. Ibid., p. 6.

149. Ibid., p. 7.

150. Ibid., p. 8.

151. Ibid., p. 16.

152. Ibid.

153. Ibid., p. 19.

154. Ibid.

155. Ibid., pp. 21-27.

156. Ibid., pp. 29-34.

157. Ibid., p. 35.

158. Ibid., pp. 34-36.

159. Pettijohn, Terry F., *Sources, Notable Selections in Psychology*, 2nd Ed. (Guilford, CT: Dushkin/McGraw-Hill, 1997), p. 327.

160. Myers, op. cit., p. 84.

161. Ibid.

162. Ibid.

163. Cialdini, op. cit., p. 92.

164. Ibid.

165. Ibid.

166. Ibid.

167. Ibid., p. 133.

168. Ibid., p. 95.

169. Ibid., p. 133.

170. Ibid.

171. Ibid.

172. Ibid., pp. 136-139.

173. Ibid, p. 169.

174. Cowley, Geoffrey, "The Biology of Beauty" in *Classic and Contemporary Readings in Social Psychology*, 3rd Ed., Edited by Eric J. Coats and Robert S. Feldman (Upper Saddle River, NJ: Pearson Education, 2001), pp. 130-131.

175. Myers, op. cit., p. 263.

176. Ibid.

177. Ibid, pp. 263-264.

178. Cialdini, op. cit., p. 169.

179. Ibid.

180. Ibid.

181. Ibid.

182. Ibid.

183. Ibid., p. 192.

184. Alex Kuczynski, " 'But Darling, It's *You*'—Invasion of the Personal Stylists, Pampered Civilians Pick up a Celebrity Habit," in *The New York Times*, Sunday, March 22, 1998, Section 9, p. 4.

185. Ibid.

186. Ibid.

187. Cialdini, op. cit., p. 192.

188. Ibid.

189. Ibid., pp. 189-190.

190. Ibid., p. 192.

191. Ibid., p. 220.

192. Ibid.

193. Ibid.

194. Ibid, p. 221.

195. Ibid., p. 229.

196. Brudnoy, David, "Bridget Jones's Diary" in *Boston Tab*, Friday, April 20, 2001, p. 6.

197. Cialdini, op. cit., p. 14.

About the Author

Jasmine Martirossian is a Boston community association homeowner and a lecturer at Northeastern University. She currently serves as secretary of the Community Associations Institute Board of Trustees and as a member of the Community Associations Institute Research Foundation's Board of Directors. She is also a frequent contributor to *Common Ground* magazine.

The author welcomes comments, personal stories and accounts, and suggestions from readers. Please contact her at jmartirossian@hotmail.com.

COMMUNITY
ASSOCIATIONS
INSTITUTE

About Community Associations Institute (CAI)

Community Associations Institute (CAI) is a national, nonprofit 501(c)(6) association created in 1973 to provide education and resources to America's 231,000 residential condominiums, cooperatives, and homeowner associations, and related professionals and service providers. The Institute is dedicated to fostering vibrant,
responsive, competent community associations that promote harmony, community,
and responsible leadership.

As a multidisciplinary alliance, CAI serves all stakeholders in community associations. CAI members include condominium and homeowner associations, cooperatives,
and association-governed planned communities of all sizes and architectural types;
individual homeowners; community association managers and management firms;
public officials; and lawyers, accountants, engineers, reserve specialists, builder/devel-
opers, and other providers of professional services and products for community associations. CAI has nearly 17,000 members in its chapters throughout the U.S. and in
several foreign countries. The national office is in Alexandria, Virginia.

How does CAI serve its members?

- CAI advances excellence through seminars, workshops, conferences, and education programs, some of which lead to professional designations.
- CAI publishes the largest collection of resources available on community associations, including books, guides, *Common Ground* magazine, and specialized newsletters on community association finance, law, and management.
- CAI advocates community association interests before legislatures, regulatory
  bodies, and the courts.
- CAI conducts research and acts as a clearinghouse of information on innova-
  tions and best practices in community association creation and management.
- CAI provides networking and referral opportunities through both the national
  office and local CAI chapters, CAI-sponsored insurance programs for directors
  and officers, a 401(k) retirement plan, and discounts on products and services.

How can I get more information on CAI or on community associations?

For membership or other information, call the national office at (703) 548-8600
(M–F, 9–5:30 ET) or visit CAI's Web site at www.caionline.org.